ACTION SPEAKS LOUDER

ELEVEN EMPOWERING STORIES
BY LEADERS IN THEIR OWN
WORDS

ENSPIRE BOOKS

ACTION SPEAKS LOUDER

#01

Published by Enspire Books

ISBN: 978-3-944681-01-6

www.enspirebooks.com

AUTHORS

FOREWORD

In the realm of entrepreneurship, where dreams collide with determination, this book stands as a beacon for those brave souls venturing into the unknown terrain of starting their own business. Within these pages lie a wealth of insights, experiences, and wisdom gathered by a diverse array of entrepreneurs who have navigated the tumultuous seas of business ownership.

Embarking on the journey of entrepreneurship is akin to setting sail on a vast ocean, where the horizon holds promise and peril in equal measure. The allure of autonomy, creativity, and financial freedom beckons many to the helm of their own enterprises. Yet, amidst the thrill of charting new territories, lie the lurking shadows of doubt, fear, and uncertainty.

Each author in this compendium has faced their own trials and tribulations, from the sleepless nights of uncertainty to the exhilarating highs of success. Through their collective narratives, they illuminate the advantages of starting their own business – the fulfillment of pursuing their passions, the freedom to innovate, the embrace of independence, and the opportunity to help and inspire others.

They also acknowledge the stark realities of the entrepreneurial journey – the risks of failure, the fear of the unknown, and the doubts that plague even the most resolute of minds. In the end, it is in confronting these challenges head-on that true growth and resilience are forged.

As you delve into the pages of this book, may you find solace in the shared experiences of those who have walked this path before you. May their stories serve as both a guiding light and a source of inspiration as you board on your own entrepreneurial odyssey. Remember, in the face of adversity, it is not the absence of fear that defines us, but rather, the courage to press onward in spite of it.

Matthias Leuschner
Founder of Enspire Books

LISA JEFFS

At 8:15 am, amidst the orchestrated chaos of Toronto's rush hour, my car was just one more piece in a sprawling mosaic of commuters. And there, amid bumper-to-bumper traffic, I was confronted with a decision that felt as much like a crossroads in my life as the congested intersection before me. It was a moment steeped in déjà vu, echoing a similar, life-altering choice I had faced a decade earlier....

Let's journey back to that moment together, so I can paint you a vivid and detailed picture...

My self-destructive trajectory began while in high school. I grappled with undiagnosed ADHD and intense anxiety, which further eroded my vulnerable self-esteem. On the surface, I projected confidence, but beneath that veneer, I was battling significant inner turmoil.

Then, with the loss of my father at 19, I was plunged into a state of confusion, hopelessness, and a profound sense of inadequacy. I struggled to envision a future where I could forge a meaningful and successful path.

A few years later, I found myself in the depths of drug addiction, and on a path that included the shadows of working in the adult entertainment industry. It was a challenging period in my life, yet one I don't regret, as it has endowed me with profound depth and insight into the human shadow — wisdom I now integrate into my work.

At age 23, I had a pivotal year marked by two life-defining events: grappling with the depths of drug addiction that had reached a rock-bottom moment and discovering I was pregnant with my daughter. The contrast of despair and hope presented two choices: continue down a path overshadowed by darkness or step into a realm of possibility and light, and become a mother.

It was an easy choice that changed everything the moment I made the decision. Pregnant with my daughter, I began to envision a future filled with hope and potential.

Transforming my life, I traded the shadows of the adult entertainment industry and drugs for a job working the night shift at a hospital coffee shop. I left behind the grip of addiction and entered each day with newfound clarity and purpose. Working at the hospital coffee shop during those quiet night shifts, I found solace in the simple yet profound interactions with people from all walks of life. Each cup of coffee served became a symbol of my journey towards healing and normalcy. The smiles I exchanged and the stories I heard were reminders of the diverse tapestry of human experiences.

In this unassuming place, I began to weave a new narrative for myself, one filled with hope, resilience, and the determination to create a future defined not by my past, but by the limitless possibilities of the present

NOW A YOUNG MOTHER…

Now, a young mother of a lively, loving toddler, I applied for college to study youth counseling. Completing the college application, I felt a profound sense of alignment with my purpose. Each stroke of the pen reinforced my belief that this was more than just a career choice; it was my calling. With my daughter's joyful presence as a constant reminder of what resilience and love can achieve, I trusted deeply in this new path. It was a commitment to guide and support young minds who needed someone to believe in them, just as I once did. This journey in youth counseling wasn't just a direction for my career; it was a manifestation of my purpose.

A few months before another defining crossroads, fast forward to my post-university days, where I landed what I thought was my dream job. This job was the beacon that had guided me through my academic journey. Yet, the reality of working in the public school system was starkly different from my idealized vision. While I was certain I was engaged in the work I was meant to do on this planet, the way I was going about it began to take its toll. The job, instead of being a dream fulfilled, was fraught with bureaucratic challenges, limited growth opportunities, and didn't allow me to support the youth in ways I knew would be effective.

The daily commute, a sluggish procession through traffic, became a metaphor for my growing disillusionment. The values and aspirations that once propelled me were now in conflict with the reality of my professional life, intensifying my anxiety and leading to a profound realization: the path I had so diligently pursued was now leading me away from my true calling. This growing awareness marked the prelude to yet another critical juncture, urging me to reassess my journey and refine my purpose.

Back to 8:15 am in my car:

And what I refer to as my 'slap in the face' moment… a day that shifted everything. It was just another morning drive to work, but it felt distinctly different. My nerves were frayed; I was exhausted, not in body or mind, but deep within my spirit.

I encountered what seemed like an energetic barrier, an insurmountable wall. In hindsight, I see it as a message from my higher self, a wake-up call of sorts. I felt as if I was aging a decade each minute, my soul withering away – dramatic, I know. But now, I recognize it as a spiritual crossroads, a pivotal moment my inner being used to show me the choices laid out before me.

I could persist in this state, enduring more days filled with anxiety, frustration, and the sense of merely surviving. Or, I could choose to change my course. That day, in my car, staring at the license plate ahead, I made a declaration – a commitment to transform my life and my daughter's future. This wasn't a mere wish or a fleeting hope; it was a solid vow, an unwavering promise to myself. I refused to spend another minute in a life that contributed to my deterioration rather than my expansion.

I've had a few such defining moments in my life, and each has heralded significant changes. The commitment I made that day was bold and powerful: I would start my own business. At that moment, I had no clear idea of what it would entail, but I was solid in my determination to make it a reality.

My new, unfolding journey began…

In the weeks that followed at the school, I found an ally in a colleague who shared my sense of disillusionment with our current roles. Together, we dove into brainstorming sessions, tossing around various business ideas. Some were far-fetched, others held potential, but nothing felt right to pursue.

The real breakthrough came when I paused and made space to do deep introspection. I took my talents, values, and lifestyle desires, and that's when it clicked – health and wellness, a realm I had been passionate about for over a decade and in which I had honed substantial expertise.

With this newfound clarity, the pieces of my future began assembling themselves rapidly. I sought the guidance of a coach, joined an online business program, and within a month, I was leading my first wellness group. Sure, it was a mix of friends and coworkers, but it was just as impactful. This experience was more than just gratifying; it was a revelation. Coaching was not just something I enjoyed but also a skill I excelled at. This synergy of joy and proficiency was a clear indication that I was moving in harmony with what I call my soul's purpose.

As my journey in coaching unfolded, so did the demographics of my clientele. Initially focusing on individual clients and small groups, I began to attract a different audience – business leaders and high-level professionals. I adapted my coaching services to meet their specific needs, creating a niche for myself.

Despite the fulfillment and joy this new path brought, there remained a part of me that clung to the security of the school board job. Opting for a supply counselor role gave me a false sense of financial backup. But deep down, I knew it was a fear-based safety net. A turning point came when the reality of going into the school, even minimally, became unbearable. It was a powerful signal from my higher self, a call to fully commit to my new path. When I received the notice of my termination from the school board, it was as if a weight had been lifted, and funny enough, my coaching business flourished like never before following the termination. I had a steady flow of new clients who came in with the organic marketing I was doing on social media and through SEO.

Embarking on this uncertain path had its share of fears, but my trust in the journey and the signs along the way never wavered. I felt supported by a higher power.

Now the support from friends and family was a mixed bag. Some found inspiration in my courage to change, while others couldn't understand why I would leave a "secure job". More strikingly, several people from my past life chose to distance themselves as I openly embraced my new direction. The loss of these connections was painful, yet it highlighted an important truth – growth often means outgrowing certain relationships. It's a part of evolving as a person. The bonds forged over shared complaints about work were no longer in line with who I was becoming. I realized personal growth is a journey that not everyone who starts with you will continue. And that's perfectly fine. As you evolve, you attract new people into your life – those who act as guiding lights, propelling you forward, rather than anchors holding you to your past.

THINGS WERE SET TO GET GOOD, REALLY GOOD AND I SABOTAGED IT ALL

The initial years of my venture were not entirely smooth sailing, but overall, they progressed quite positively. I enjoyed a steady influx of clients, my social media presence was blossoming, and my voice found a place in several renowned publications. I was frequently invited to speak at events or contribute to exciting projects. Mentally, I was in a place of strength and confidence, optimistic about the future I was shaping.

However, as plans for a major expansion of my business began to develop for the following year, something shifted within me. This impending growth unearthed a part of me that shied away from the spotlight, hesitant to be seen or heard on such a grand scale. I felt myself withdrawing, caught in a surreal dichotomy: part of me eager to advance, the other part desperately pulling back.

I spiraled into self-sabotage which looked like me, procrastinating on projects, and overthinking everything I was putting out. And a multitude of other behaviors to stall my growth. Compounding this was the lack of understanding from some peers and mentors. Their well-intentioned advice to simply 'suck it up and take action' was more harmful than helpful. I believe in the value of tough love, especially when we become entangled in our stories. But what I was experiencing, which I can now identify as a trauma response, required a different approach. The 'suck it up' mentality not only failed to address my state, but it also instilled a sense of guilt and shame for not being able to 'just figure things out.'

I found myself overwhelmed and in deep, consuming frustration. When I launched my business, I operated with a natural boldness and clarity. My offers were made effortlessly, my writings were unfiltered expressions of my thoughts, and I acted with courage and conviction.

So why this drastic change now?

In hindsight, I realize there's a unique confidence that accompanies the early stages of a business. There's power in having little to lose. With a small audience and fewer clients, it's easier to be daring and take risks.

However, once you've established yourself, it's a different ballgame. Success brings its challenges – it's a double-edged sword. The very achievements that elevate you can also be the ones that create new fears and pressures.

It's important to understand that such challenges are often less a matter of actual truth and more about personal perception. My fears about judgment from others, if I got super well-known, were rooted far more in the tales I spun in my mind than in any real external judgment. However this didn't make them any less impactful at the time, nor did it lessen their paralyzing effect on my life and business.

The catalyst for change came during a session with one of my spiritual mentors. She looked at me and said, 'You know, Lisa, I think you've just forgotten who you are.' That statement resonated deeply, echoing in my mind for days. I mulled over it, turning it this way and that, until yes, it was clear... I had indeed forgotten who I was.

More than just a problem solver, I am a force to be reckoned with. Having turned my life around completely after four years of intense drug addiction and the shadows of the adult entertainment industry, I knew I had the strength to overcome this phase of self-sabotage. I was ready to embrace the growth and expansion my life and business were destined for.

Thus began a journey of about one and a half years, learning and healing. To not just to apply a temporary fix to self-sabotage, but to free myself from it entirely. This process also became a key framework in supporting my clients.

At the heart of it, I discovered that sabotaging progress in your business stems from feelings of lack of safety or unworthiness. The growth of my business had reawakened old fears of not being safe to fully express myself, and it stirred dormant feelings of inadequacy.

Business, I realized, has a unique way of bringing all our hidden challenges to the surface. It's a journey that's as much about personal discovery as it is about professional success.

One of the most challenging aspects of healing and deep personal growth is that it often intensifies before it improves.

A turning point in my journey to free myself from self-sabotage emerged after a workshop I conducted...

The event itself went smoothly, but my message wasn't tailored to the right audience. They were expecting a more laid-back session, whereas my approach was akin to how I interact with my entrepreneurial clients – a slight misalignment. Despite this, the workshop wasn't bad, but my inner critic launched a relentless attack, chastising me for perceived failures. As it dug it's claws in there was a part of me that felt like an observer, detached and witnessing the reality of the situation from the sidelines. It allowed me to distinguish my true self from the deceptive narratives spun by my inner critic. This revelation was powerful. It showed me that as you work towards liberation the parts of you trying to keep you safe might work harder.

This increase in volume doesn't equate to truth. An amplified inner critic doesn't wield more power than one operating subtly in the background; its influence is only as strong as the power we assign to it...

After the workshop, I decided to watch my thoughts as an observer instead of getting caught up in the negativity from my inner critic. This change was a big deal: it weakened the hold of my inner critic and brought me closer to feeling truly free.

The voice of your inner saboteur/critic isn't meant to turn your life or business endeavors into overwhelming struggles. Its true purpose is to protect you. By adopting the role of an observer and getting curious about why your inner saboteur or critic is intensifying, you can prevent becoming entangled in its web. This detachment allows you to view these internal dialogues through a lens of completeness and begin addressing the underlying concerns it's trying to shield you from.

In my journey, a significant part of my healing involved addressing fears of judgment. I focused on increasing my self-esteem and nurturing the aspects of my younger self that felt compelled to overachieve to prove her worth. I reached a place of intrinsic self-worth, recognizing that my value comes simply from being me – something that no one can take away. This realization affirmed that I was complete and safe to embrace expansion and growth.

That's not to say I never have moments of apprehension or times when my inner critic chirps in. This is part of being a human being. However, these moments of doubt now serve as reminders of my growth, rather than barriers to my progress. I recognize them as fleeting thoughts, not definitions of my capability. Today, I stand firm in my power, confidently crafting a life and business brimming with purpose and prosperity. My journey has taught me resilience, and each day is a testament to the unyielding strength and wisdom that lies within me.

OUR DREAMS ARE OURS FOR A REASON

I firmly believe that we all have a purpose here on this planet. This purpose isn't confined to a single career or job. Instead, it's about bringing our authentic selves forward and honoring our dreams. When we have a persistent dream or desire, it's there for a reason – in this world, there are no coincidences.

Take, for example, my clients George and Janet (Real names changed for confidentiality). They're a married couple who have successfully grown and are still growing a YouTube channel and a video game development company. George had aspired to be a video game developer since he was 12, but he initially chose a more conventional career path, one considered 'safer' by societal standards. However, he wasn't fulfilled. When George first came to me he expressed a desire to start his own coaching practice.

However when I introduced him to a 'highest intention meditation,' (a technique I use with clients to connect with their higher selves for guidance). George received a clear message to pursue his game development venture.

He didn't hesitate or second-guess this insight; the clarity of the message instilled a deep sense of trust. Together, George and Janet, both natural entrepreneurs, dove headfirst into this new venture. They were consistent, adapted as they learned, and soon gained significant momentum. Their channel and business continue to flourish. A key to this success was their belief in themselves and the understanding that they were following a path meant for them.

One critical aspect of launching a new venture is the unwavering belief in your ability to succeed. You don't need to have every step figured out, but a strong belief in yourself is essential. Any doubts can grow insidiously, affecting your decisions and clouding your judgment.

Reading biographies can be a fantastic source of inspiration, especially those about individuals who have risen from challenging beginnings to achieve remarkable success.

Reflecting on my own 'slap-in-the-face' moment while driving to work, at the time I didn't fully comprehend the extent to which my business would grow, the amazing clients I would have the privilege to work with, or the incredible global connections and adventures that lay ahead. All I knew was that I couldn't continue on the same path and that the challenges I had faced and overcome in my youth were for a reason. And that reason included me leaving an impact on this world.

Launching my coaching and speaking business has expanded my horizons beyond anything I could have originally imagined. This journey has propelled me into a world of deeper fulfillment and unprecedented opportunities, surpassing even my wildest dreams. And I'm only getting started!

LETTING GO OF THE TIES THAT BIND US

Fears are a normal part of being a human being. If we didn't have fears, we'd be walking out in front of traffic and engaging in reckless behaviors without any regard for our safety or well-being.

However, many of the fears we hold about pursuing our dreams are unfounded and don't have to be roadblocks. Instead, they can serve as stepping stones that we navigate through. My hope for you is to give yourself the freedom to explore your deepest desires and the whispers of your heart. These calls might not always seem logical at first, but often, it's only when we look back on our lives that their true meaning becomes clear.

A few questions you may find helpful to ponder

01. What specific fears do I have about starting this business, and what can I do to address each one?

02. How have I successfully dealt with fear or uncertainty in the past, and how can those experiences inform my current situation?

03. What is the worst that could happen, and how would I cope with or recover from that scenario?

04. What are the potential rewards of starting this business, and how do they compare to my fears?

05. If fear were not a factor, what bold steps would I take right now?

Your dreams are the echoes of your true purpose, waiting to be realized. Trust in the journey, believe in your power, and know that each step, no matter how tentative, is a leap towards a life of fulfillment and true success. Your path may not always be clear or easy, but it is uniquely yours, rich with opportunities to leave a permanent mark on the world. So go forth with courage, armed with the knowledge that within you lies an unstoppable force, ready to transform your dreams into reality.

LISA JEFFS is a certified coach of over a decade, professional intuitive, transformational speaker and host of The Confident Connected Leader Podcast. Her movement SHEspires is here to empower women, showing them not just how to live up to their potential but how to redefine it and make waves in a world needing change. Her insights and voice have illuminated a variety of platforms, such as The National Post, Bumble Bizz, Toronto 640 Talk Radio, Tiny Buddha, and Thrive Global, to name a few. She's Toronto-born, adores her family and her very rambunctious tortoise, Tortellini!

Instagram: *https://www.instagram.com/lisa_jeffs*
Facebook: *https://www.facebook.com/lisajeffscoach/*
LinkedIn: *https://www.linkedin.com/in/lisajeffs/*
Website: *lisajeffs.com*
            lisajeffsglobal.com

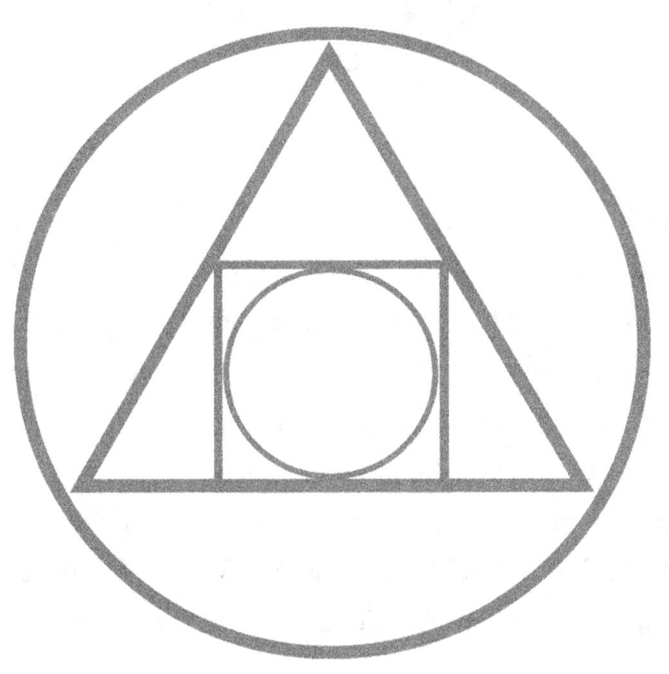

SIMONE IBRAHIM

When I look back on my old life, I immediately sense this deep sadness that accompanied me throughout all the years of my childhood, youth, and early adulthood. Though I was never depressed, generally quite positive towards life, always had a good sense of humor, and often initiated various adventures and creations with my adventurous spirit. But beneath it all, there was this weight, and sadness lingered like the dark waters hidden deep below the surface. From an outsider's perspective, I had achieved quite a bit in my life: a master's degree in communication science, married my high school sweetheart, bought a great house, secured a stable job, and had long-lasting friendships. Nonetheless, I always felt somewhat lost in this world, as if I were strangely alien here with no truly fitting place for me. All that is conveyed as meaningful in life didn't genuinely bring me happiness. Since my early childhood, I was bored, and as I grew older, the depth of my soul felt increasingly unfulfilled. My only real passion was traveling, any forms of aesthetics, social connections, and exploring and expanding my own consciousness.

As a teenager, at the age of 16, during the first real crisis in my life, I reached a nadir of meaninglessness. My family had just broken apart, I was experiencing terrible heartbreak, I was immensely bored with school, and my professional future was a big question mark since none of the possibilities truly interested me. When I began meditating at the age of 17, I experienced a deep sense of enthusiasm for the first time. I felt a new connection with myself, a reminder of who I truly am. I had many consciousness-expanding experiences, encounters with beings from other dimensions, and insights into other worlds and levels of being. My inner spark was ignited. For many years, I remained faithful to this meditation practice, creating a space for deep self-encounter.

While it was helpful in one aspect, my studies and subsequently my work in the professional world seemed even more meaningless to me. I was underwhelmed and still utterly bored. So, my focus was mainly on my personal life as I sought meaning within it. I wanted to start a family with my then-husband. Unfortunately, it didn't work out; even after 5 years, I hadn't become pregnant. At some point during this time, we discovered that my partner couldn't conceive. This shattered my world, and I suffered immensely. I felt like I had failed and couldn't comprehend it. I was angry at life and felt so powerless. In hindsight, I know something crucial was set in motion. I began asking myself important questions. In my frustration, I even posed questions to the unborn child: "What's the problem?", "Why don't you want to be born?", "What am I doing wrong?", "What do you need from me?", "Why are you even here?" To all these questions, I received one very important answer: "Before you can give me life, you must give it to yourself." This sentence triggered a lot within me.

I had to admit how unfulfilled I was, in my work and in my relationship within this traditional Western life model. So, one day, the question arose within me, "Who am I if I lose everything?" This question came with great force and clarity. I felt that everything was about to change for me. There was no other way but to face the answer to this question.

A few weeks later, I separated from my husband and moved out of our shared house. I fell into a deep hole, cried a lot. Simultaneously, I had started training as a Psychosynthesis Counselor, which helped me clarify, remember, integrate, and heal deep wounds within me. I found a way to connect and align the strong and essential link to my essence, the spiritual world, and the broader field of consciousness with my humanity, personality, and body – something crucial for me. It became increasingly clear who I truly am, and I began shedding the layers of programming and masks I had adopted. I gathered courage, developed self-love, self-worth, self-confidence, and gained more and more inner clarity. Despite the chaos in my external life – temporarily living on a friend's couch, having an unsatisfying connection with another man, struggling to focus at work, and emotionally navigating through all the traumas of my childhood – there was still a clear direction internally. And that direction pointed inward. It was genuinely not an easy time. Life demanded everything from me, leading me to a point where, in all aspects, the only choice I had was to commit to the best possible relationship with myself and painfully let go of all external securities.

Unable to endure my job any longer, I requested a 4-week unpaid leave, which was denied. Consequently, without anything else on the horizon or a clear sense of direction, I resigned.

I ended the relationship with the man who didn't know what he wanted, even though I was drawn to him like a magnet. Emotionally, I found myself in my own hell, confronting my own demons. I struggled with the internal dragon, dealing with pain, powerlessness, and a sense of directionlessness. A very real feeling of dissolution or death overcame me repeatedly. While trying to resist these internal and external deaths, I reached a point where I simply couldn't anymore. And I gave up.

It happened at night in my bed. I felt that I had no strength left; it pulled me deeper into those dark waters, the inner blackness. It became tighter, heavier, the emotional pain stronger; I cried bitterly. And I just let it happen. Then suddenly, it became calm. It was like turning the inside of a garment outward. There was only light and peace. The whole room was filled with this light, and I could see nothing else. A fire ignited in my lower back, slowly moving up my spine, pausing at each energy centre (chakra), flooding it with burning heat. It was uncomfortable and beautiful simultaneously. My body twitched. Then, I couldn't feel my arms anymore; they became immobile and numb. My whole body buzzed as if electricity flowed through me. I was in a state of timelessness and bliss, and at some point, I must have fallen asleep. The days that followed were not easy.

I cried continuously for three days. And I could do nothing. I just lay on the bed and cried. Eventually, it got better, and I began to understand what had happened to me. What I had experienced was a spontaneous Kundalini awakening. What I didn't know at that time was that this energy would release and flow through me several more times. All the immense tension in my body, which had hardened over the past few weeks, was gone. I was in absolute trust with my life, knowing that I had just gone through a turning point. For two years, this energy would rise again and again, causing significant pain in my body afterward, difficulties grounding myself, many transpersonal experiences, feeling partially completely disconnected from the world as I perceived everything from a completely different perspective. Alongside this, there were tremendous surges of releasing emotions, painful realizations, but at the same time, an unwavering trust in myself and my life. A feeling of absolute security that I would always be taken care of. These experiences opened up even deeper connections to the Divine, to creation, to the cosmos, but also to being human. For the entire two years, I spent several hours daily in nature and lived extremely withdrawn. I aligned myself internally with an entirely new life. It was as if I had died and was now reborn, without ever leaving my body.

Now it was time to start my real work. Since I was about 20 years old, I knew that one day I would work with people and help them remember who they truly are and what they could do to create a life aligned with that. However, all these years since my late youth, I also knew that I wasn't ready yet. I lacked life experience; I was simply too young. The only thing I started around the age of 27 was leading meditations and groups for consciousness training. I kept it somewhat hidden, thinking that people important to me might ridicule or even condemn it. At that time, I wasn't internally strong and free enough to confidently follow my own path, regardless of others' opinions.

Now, after this intense time of metamorphosis that initiated me to start the work that truly fulfilled me, where I could be completely myself, I felt ready. There was no doubt that now was the right time. Of course, the decision brought a lot of new doubts with it.

'Will anyone even be interested in what I offer?'

'What if I can't make a living from it?'

'What if I'm not good enough?'

'What if I'm not visible enough?'

'What if my clients are dissatisfied with my work?'

So, while I created a website and business cards, I still didn't fully launch. I simply didn't know how or where to begin.

As my funds slowly depleted, life applied the necessary pressure, pushing me to find the drive to apply at all the yoga studios in the city where I lived at that time, offering meditation and yoga classes. This opened doors to three studios, introducing me to a new environment and people I hadn't known before. Positive feedback from participants quickly emerged, leading to my first clients. One participant wanted to purchase a package of 10 sessions, and others recommended my services. I received a request to provide meditation classes for a company during their lunch break. Surprisingly, I was chosen as the instructor from among various applicants. Since it was a corporate setting, I confidently set a substantial fee for these sessions, gaining assurance in sharing my work with strangers. This gradually led me into my journey of self-employment. However, my counseling and coaching sessions weren't heavily booked yet. Fortunately, other coaches, yoga teachers, and individuals involved in consciousness work started approaching me to get to know me, befriend me, and exchange ideas. This was immensely helpful. Everyone was in the process of building their own businesses, and we shared insights on what worked for us in promoting our work. This led me to try running a Google ad, bringing in new clients who didn't know me from my personal network or yoga studio classes.

That's how the small seed slowly began to grow.

There wasn't much interest or encouragement regarding my work from my personal circle, with a few exceptions. I didn't let this discourage me; instead, I spent more time with new friends and acquaintances who showed interest in my work. For me, there was no turning back. I enjoyed being able to do what truly brought me joy and where I excelled. I consciously avoided overcommitting myself during this initial phase. It was and still is crucial for me not to create a new prison where I constantly have to prove myself. I have a business, but I am not my business. My business is meant to nourish me, bring me joy, help me grow, challenge me – but not define, exhaust, or overwhelm me. I know this responsibility lies solely with me. So, I still had plenty of time for myself and other essential aspects of my life.

In the beginning, I was consistently challenged in terms of my relationship with clients. I learned to set clear boundaries and endure uncomfortable situations. With each experience, I grew into my new role. My willingness to learn and grow was always present.

What posed more difficulty for me was the entire marketing aspect. Despite my knowledge in the field, it was challenging for myself. Firstly, because I can't hide behind my company – my persona represents the business. Secondly, I distance myself from traditional marketing strategies that employ sales psychology resembling a toxic relationship. I don't want to manipulate my clients in a subtle way, even though I know how to do it. Nevertheless, I find ways to authentically make myself visible without compromising important values such as integrity, honesty, empathy, freedom, and balance, just to feel financially secure or successful.

Trusting that people will find me and choose to work with me requires a considerable amount of trust. I draw this trust from the deep faith in life that I've developed. I am willing to experience failure and losses in life repeatedly because I trust in my ability to handle them. I believe there's a path for me that doesn't require me to fight fiercely or betray my values. Internally, I often speak to my higher consciousness:

'Guide me.'

'Show me where you want me to be.'

'Direct me to the right place and the right people at the right time.'

'Create opportunities and open doors for me.'

'I promise to give my all wherever you lead me.'

Beyond trusting my path, what I continually prove are: my joy in the work, the ability to embrace change and growth, holding onto my values, summoning the will to take action at the right moment, and knowing when to do nothing and let go. I make sure not to act out of fear and to release rigid expectations about how things should unfold or the precise forms my business and I should take. Sometimes, things happen entirely differently than we could have imagined. This was the case for me when a highly satisfied client recommended me to 'Younity' (a publisher in the field of spirituality and personal development). After an interview, I got the opportunity to speak at two conferences with a significant reach. We even collaborated on a course together, opening many doors for me. Subsequently, I was invited as a speaker to more conferences, expanding my reach from Switzerland to the entire German-speaking region.

In the midst of the COVID-19 crisis, I transitioned from an offline to an online business, becoming a digital nomad virtually overnight. I decided to ride the wave of success that rolled through my life during this time, slightly increasing my prices and working extensively. Today, I realise it might have been a bit too much, as I almost lost the joy in my work due to not retaining enough energy for myself. This experience helped me disengage from identifying too closely with success, bringing me back to a place where success is irrelevant, and asking myself important questions about simplifying processes, determining how much I genuinely want to work to maintain balance, what I want to continue offering, and what I might need to let go. The opportunity presented by 'Younity' had urged me to plunge into the unknown, expose myself to broad public opinion, and deliver a lot in a short time. Although I generally enjoy challenges, it wasn't always a comfortable journey. Afterward, I felt the desire not to become too dependent on individual business partners and to make myself visible through as many channels as possible. I always follow what brings me joy, avoiding anything that feels like I have to do it, but it doesn't align with who I am. It might take a bit longer at times, but that's okay for me.

What I truly want to achieve with my work is not to prove something, but to do something that genuinely fulfils me in a way that keeps me in balance. I also aim to create financial abundance with my business without engaging in activities that compromise my integrity. After all, this is what I teach my clients, and I stand for what I teach – embodying it. The quality of my work is paramount to me, and it truly pays off. My clients are wonderful individuals willing to take responsibility for themselves and their values. Through our work, they develop the courage, balance, and awareness to live their lives authentically, free from external morals, concepts, and structures defining who they should be and how they should live. What brings me immense joy in my work is witnessing these individuals become internally liberated, cultivating more self-love and self-confidence, resulting in increased trust in themselves and their lives. This positive transformation also extends to all their relationships – with people, their professions, and life itself. I see these as crucial collective developmental steps for the evolution of our society:

How can we learn to be fully ourselves while simultaneously establishing deep connections with others and the world around us?

How can we embrace the beauty of the world without turning away from its darkness and suffering?

How can we consistently restore balance even when life moves up and down, left and right?

How can we learn to love ourselves exactly as we are, while still embracing change, growth, and improvement?

I witness daily how this brings so much more inner peace, relaxation, and a greater sense of ease and joy in life. I have clients experiencing things they describe as miracles—synchronicities, unexpected opportunities, and shifts in their jobs and relationships—simply because they learn to truly let go and realign themselves.

I teach them things we have never learned in school

How universal laws function and how to work with them.

How to handle our emotions constructively.

How to connect with our essence and inner wisdom.

How to reprogram the subconscious and heal traumas.

How to navigate and utilize different roles in life.

How to hold polarities and paradoxes within us.

How to truly embody our bodies and become more coherent within ourselves.

It's more of a life school than just coaching, and it's my greatest passion.

That my passion contributes to creating something that not only helps individuals live coherently but also breaks through collective patterns leading to imbalance in our society gives my work a profound sense of purpose. I find that incredibly meaningful.

I understand each unique path of my clients as valuable, enriching, challenging, and perfectly right in its uniqueness, just as I feel towards my own journey. It's neither better nor worse than any other path—it's mine, and no one else should walk it except me. This path has led me to numerous insights, a high level of consciousness, and wisdom. I naturally want to share these with others so that it may serve them on their own journeys. I truly have no regrets about anything I've been through; it has shaped me into who I am today, and I appreciate myself as I am. Life is eternal change, and I am aware that my business will evolve as well. Currently, what I love most about my work is guiding people one-on-one. Working with many over extended periods brings me great joy, as we get to know each other well and delve deep to address issues at their roots, creating lasting change. I've noticed that our vulnerability, fears, and weaknesses are essential parts of the beauty within us, akin to flowers whose beauty lies not only in their mystical outward force but also in the delicacy of their blossoms. I also immensely enjoy writing and speaking about topics important to me and answering questions. If I could offer one piece of advice for people to enjoy life more, it would be: Remember who you truly are at your essence and develop the courage, love, and trust to align your life accordingly. This requires facing both your light and darkness, as only together do they make you whole. In this wholeness lies an unshakable power that creates from within and attracts what truly aligns with you.

This inner abundance will naturally extend to your external life, including your business or any other significant life plans you might have. It's normal not to have a clue about how you'll reach your goal at the beginning—the path reveals itself as you walk it. You just have to take the steps yourself.

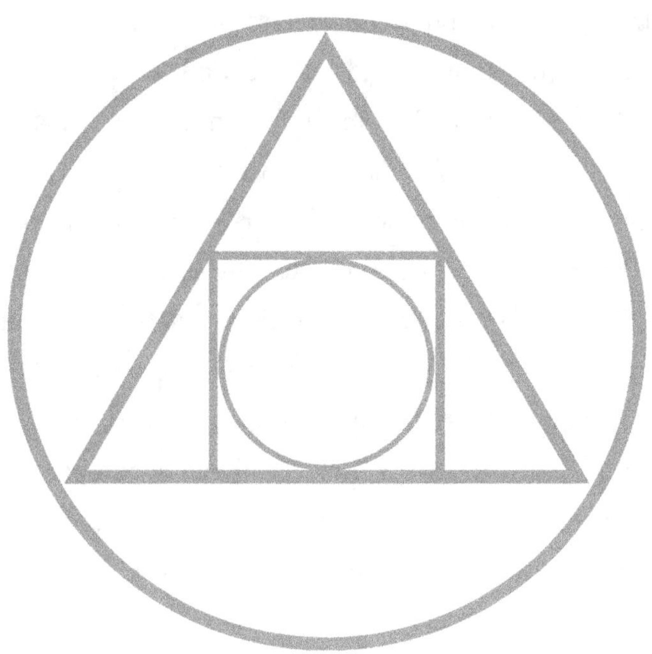

SIMONE IBRAHIM discovered her psychic abilities as a teenager, had many transpersonal and consciousness-expanding experiences, and remembered a reality that extends far beyond the sensory perceptible dimension. At the age of 33, she left behind her previous life and experienced a spontaneous Kundalini awakening in the midst of a deep crisis, which led her through several years of profound transformation and expansion of consciousness. Her calling is to guide people through phases of transformation and to help them anchor themselves in the heart. This is achieved through awareness, inner healing, and integration, leading to a new, more coherent inner order. She reminds us of the inherent creative power within us all and accompanies those who wish to live in a more conscious, harmonious, and connected way. In her courses and 1:1 sessions, she integrates transpersonal psychology, Egyptian alchemy, AWBD body therapy, and energy work. Since 2022, she has been living in Egypt.

Instagram: *_simone.ibrahim_*
Website: *www.simoneibrahim.com*

DR ROBIN LAVITCH

THE OPPORTUNITY

I vividly recall preparing for a meeting with the company owner. My boss had instructed me to meet him at Panera (a place I hadn't even heard of back then) because he wanted to discuss my business background. I was thoroughly perplexed; after all, what business background did I have? Why did he want to meet with me? I felt a mixture of confusion and intimidation that made it hard to find a comfortable spot in my own skin. The owner was remarkably successful, juggling several businesses, and exuded an undeniable charm. He had a solid business background, having successfully managed a construction business and multiple social service agencies alongside his wife, who focused on raising their children while he led the agencies. At the time, I was working in one of his agencies as an independent contractor, serving as an in-home counselor for foster care kids.

I had earned a reputation as the counselor who could truly make a difference for troubled kids when others struggled. Yet, I never quite grasped the compliments and accolades. This wasn't the first time I'd received such feedback; I'd heard similar praises in my previous role as a counselor for teen runaways at a shelter. Prior to that, I had worked in a locked-down facility for teenage girls. I was just a couple of years out of school, armed with my Master's in Developmental Psychology, and on the path toward my doctorate. However, I battled severe imposter syndrome, resorting to drugs and alcohol as coping mechanisms.

Deep down, I firmly believed that the graduate school had made a mistake accepting me and that they would eventually realize their error and expel me. My upbringing in a dysfunctional family had left me with a persistent feeling of inadequacy. I was tenacious in my pursuit, but beneath the surface, I felt broken. During my pursuit of a master's degree, I hadn't been sober for a single day. It all spiraled out of control, leading me to rehab after quitting school and my job in my mid-twenties.

After my journey to sobriety, I began applying for jobs that were incidentally in the counseling field. My graduate education had revolved around scientific research, and I hadn't taken a single counseling course. My passion lay in understanding why some individuals could overcome abuse and violence, a concept now known as resilience. Ironically, while I delved into such a topic academically, my personal life was on a downward trajectory. Thankfully, my self-sabotaging tendencies only persisted for a few years, allowing me to rebound quickly.

Eventually, I found myself counseling kids facing remarkably similar challenges. However, I couldn't shake the feeling of being an untrained counselor. For the time being, I was content as long as they were satisfied with my performance.

I juggled my role at the runaway shelter with another position as an independent contractor for another agency, supplementing my income. I had a salaried job that paid $28,000 despite eight years of education, a fact that bewildered me. On the other hand, as an independent contractor, I was earning $48 per hour, and it felt like hitting the jackpot. Eventually, I left the shelter to focus more on counseling contracts.

Still in my late twenties and only a couple of years sober, I was approached by the director to consider another contract position as a case coordinator. My role involved matching foster care kids in need of treatment with contract counselors based on their location and expertise. I eagerly accepted the role, though it was initially supposed to be five hours per week, it quickly expanded to 15 hours.

Within a few weeks, I found myself contemplating how to convince them to establish a management position for the program. There had been some internal drama, leading to the removal of another program manager. The company had decided to save costs by outsourcing some roles, which left me feeling puzzled. Foster care kids urgently needed counseling, and we had a waiting list. The children weren't receiving help, and the company wasn't making money. I had ideas, so I shared them with my boss, who asked me to draft a proposal. I don't know exactly what I suggested, but it made sense to me that there should be a win-win solution.

Subsequently, she presented my ideas to the owner, which led to a meeting to explore my supposed business background. In reality, I had no business background. I had been immersed in psychology research while battling my personal demons. When the owner inquired about my business background, I stumbled, except for mentioning that both my parents were entrepreneurs, so I must have picked up something from them. My father was highly successful in marketing and other unconventional ventures, while my mother was an artist and cosmetologist.

My sole business experience, at the age of nine, involved selling candy (real candy – sugar!) to my schoolmates. My parents were divorced, and I'd go to the local candy store to pack my lunch. One day, a kid spotted my watermelon Jolly Rancher and desperately wanted it, offering to pay for it. I attended a prestigious private school on a hill, and access to candy was scarce, making the kids there crave it even more. I wasn't about to part with my Jolly Rancher lunch, so I promised to bring one for him the next day. Another student overheard and wanted to place an order too. So, I asked them for their flavor preferences, took notes, and bought the candies that evening. I returned to school the next day with my $0.10 candies, charged $0.20 each, and they gave me a quarter, telling me to keep the change. More orders followed, and my mom suggested I ask the store clerk if I could get a bulk discount. I created a table to track orders and made daily deliveries. One day, a classmate pulled me out of class to place an order, and the teacher, astonished by the sudden buzz around my candy business, asked, "Are you the one selling candy?" Apparently, some parents had complained about their children's sugar intake at school, and my candy enterprise came to an abrupt halt. That was the extent of my business experience.

I couldn't provide answers to questions about my job experience, training, or education. There simply wasn't any. When asked how I had come up with the business proposal, I had no concrete response; it just seemed like common sense. Why wouldn't we serve those in need and make a profit?

As it turned out, the business meeting, which essentially amounted to an interview, apparently went well. I was subsequently promoted to program director, essentially creating a position for myself based on identifying the needs of our clients and the agency.

In just three years, I managed to secure six promotions, eventually landing the role of Vice President of Programs. I became second-in-command to the owner, despite my limited leadership and business experience. I wrote grants, developed new programs, oversaw five departments, managed 40 independent contractors, and handled the company's marketing. If a task was necessary, I took it on willingly.

By the time I reached thirty, I was earning a six-figure salary and dedicating 80 to 100 hours a week to prove my worth and become indispensable.

THE COST

Even though I was putting in immense effort, I realized I wasn't well-suited for the role, and I certainly wasn't qualified for the next stage.

The owner had an idea to transform a non-profit social service agency into a for-profit one, aiming to transfer its assets and eventually sell it. He brought in a new director who would become my boss, positioning him to grow and sell the company. They presented me with another opportunity: a partnership. In my new contract, I would be compensated based on company growth and shares, essentially structured like a sales commission with a promising payout. I thought this was incredible.

In just six months, we managed to grow the agency from $3 million to $6 million. With all this growth, one would expect us to be living the high life. However, the reality was quite different. We struggled to pay contractors and vendors on time, and we were hemorrhaging money left and right.

The director and I embarked on a mission to understand what was happening. Our practice was to bill Medicaid for as much as possible, so where was all the money going? We tried to obtain answers from the main partner and the accountant, only to discover that a significant amount of the billed money wasn't being paid due to data entry errors. We streamlined our systems, downsized, and continued to build the agency.

Meanwhile, the main partner was driving a top-of-the-line Mercedes as well as his new girlfriend and he even had a private plane. We found ourselves struggling to support foster care parents during the holidays and had to cut out all company events to save money. I was utterly mystified – what was happening to the money? How could this be?

Every day, I fielded calls from people demanding their payments, listened to staff complaints, and racked my brain trying to find solutions. Then, we received notice of a Medicaid audit, my worst fear. I was worried they would discover mistakes, and we'd have to repay money we didn't even have. During preparations for the audit, the owner suggested that we falsify records and make sure everything appeared in order to avoid paybacks. I timidly pointed out that signing documents with backdates and such was illegal, expressing my discomfort with such actions (I'm still not sure how I found the courage to do so).

I was responsible for overseeing five of the six programs. The one program with the most issues, the cash cow, was the one I didn't manage. Instead, I focused on reviewing documents and maintaining integrity and honesty.

Slowly, the pieces of the puzzle started falling into place, and I realized there was no money because the company was funding the owner's plane, gas, vehicles, trips, and more. I was beside myself and knew that this situation would drive me to drink. How could someone steal money from foster care kids? I was horrified. Eventually, a company was found to purchase the agency, and I made the decision to leave with no plan or backup. I believed that my sobriety and principles were worth more than staying in that environment. They proceeded with the merger, and later, they were sued for Medicaid fraud, but only on the one program I hadn't overseen.

I had no idea what my next step would be, but the thought of returning to being a counselor after everything I had learned about business felt disappointing. It was in 2006 when two people independently suggested that I should become a coach. At first, I was puzzled; "a coach," I thought, "like a baseball or soccer coach?" I had no desire for that. They clarified - a life coach. I don't believe in coincidences, so the fact that I heard the same suggestion within a matter of weeks made me think there might be something to it. I conducted research and immediately knew that was the path I wanted to take.

THE PLAN

Becoming a coach felt like the perfect fusion of helping people and integrating business principles. It resonated with me as the path I was meant to follow. With coaching, I could establish my own company and run it ethically. I could maintain a good standard of living while making a meaningful difference. It was the opportunity to create the life I had always envisioned. This was the path I had chosen, and I was determined to make it work.

I delved into researching various coaching schools and embarked on setting up my own coaching business. I had some familiarity with business setup from our experience with the for-profit social service agency. Surely, I thought, I already possessed the necessary knowledge to do this.

One day, I walked into Barnes and Noble (remarkably, the same store still exists!). I gathered every book on business planning and development I could find. The stack of books grew so high that I had to use my chin to steady it. The cashier gave me an incredulous look, as if she couldn't fathom anyone reading them all. But I was determined. I poured over each book, marking them with highlights, notes, and tabs. I explored topics like business structure, QuickBooks, budgeting (especially the accounting part), marketing, and planning.

In May 2006, I officially started my coaching business, and in August of that same year, I enrolled in a certification program for coaching. I would often sit in my pajamas (a habit I still maintain!) and meticulously craft a comprehensive game plan. I even created an organizational chart with my name in every box! I developed my own policies and procedures, crafted a long-term vision and strategy, conducted market research, and pieced together every aspect, including the identification of my competitive advantage. My initial goal was ambitious - to return to earning six figures within just six months. However, I soon realized that I needed clients to turn my business dream into reality. The question that loomed large was, "How the heck do you get clients?"

THE CHALLENGE

Every business book I read emphasized the importance of building a business through networking and relationships. However, I had no idea how to do that, and honestly, the idea of networking didn't appeal to me at all. So, I reluctantly attended my first Chamber of Commerce meeting, which happened to be after hours at a bar. Now, here's the twist—I'm a sober introvert. Talk about a fun evening. I was utterly clueless about how to schmooze, how to talk about my business, how to connect with others, or even how to make small talk. I felt like I might vomit at any moment. As soon as I could manage without making it too obvious, I made a hasty exit, vowing never to attend another 'mixer' again.

But here was the conundrum: how do you build a business without networking? None of the books I read offered a marketing strategy for introverts. Everywhere I turned, attending events, mixers, and "getting out there" seemed to be the prevailing theme. The problem was, I was terrible at it. Really terrible.

At the time, my boyfriend had his own appliance repair company and was invited to a networking event by a mutual friend. He was open to the idea but suggested it might be more up my alley. So, I began to inquire about this BNI (Business Networking International) event. It was early in the morning and structured, with an agenda and a process for networking. This seemed a bit more manageable, so I decided to give it a shot. I attended the meeting, awkwardly as can be, but I found it somewhat tolerable. Additionally, there was an educational component that actually taught us how to network effectively. I thought, "I can do this." So, I joined BNI just one month after starting my coaching business. I was apprehensive about acquiring new clients since I hadn't even completed my training yet. However, I believed that by the time I had developed relationships, communicated what I do, and truly knew people, I'd be ready.

I attended that meeting every week and joined every other networking event I could fit into my schedule. I invested a considerable amount of time and money into networking, to the point where I wondered how I would find time to see clients. I took the first step by working with a pro bono client, which allowed me to collect testimonials. I continued on this challenging journey, managing to secure a couple of clients after several months. Still, it wasn't enough to support me, and my ambitious goal of achieving success within six months was rapidly approaching, with no sight of reaching it. I soon realized that starting a business from scratch was a far cry from marketing an established business with key employees. I had been naive enough to venture into this, but I wasn't sure if I was smart or persistent enough to succeed.

My confidence plummeted, and to make matters worse, my boyfriend and I parted ways. It was an amicable separation, but I was uncertain if I could afford to continue living in my house. Even if I secured a 'regular' job, it might not be enough to cover my bills. I felt like a complete failure in both my personal relationship and my career. We came to an agreement: we would live together in separate rooms for six months. If, by the end of that period, I couldn't make my business work, I'd find a job and decide whether I had to sell the house and move. Months passed, and I still wasn't making the progress I had hoped for. I started browsing job postings, updated my resume, and questioned my entire existence. During a holiday visit with my family, while sitting in a hotel room, I experienced a complete breakdown. I had done everything I needed to do, yet nothing seemed to be working. I didn't know what else to try; I felt utterly lost, and my life was in turmoil.

In that moment of despair, I picked up a book, and in bold italics (whether it was real or not), I read the line: 'God's delay is not God's denial.' I began to cry even harder but then had a revelation. Just because I had set out to achieve my goals within a year didn't mean it had to happen exactly on my timeline. Sometimes things are delayed, but that doesn't mean they won't happen eventually. I contemplated deeply. Is this truly what I want to do? Is this my calling? And for the first time, I felt an unwavering conviction. Yes, this is what I'm meant to do. I could feel it in my bones, with every fiber of my being. This was my purpose. So, now what? What was I supposed to do?

With newfound determination, I turned over a notepad and began brainstorming a multitude of ideas on how to generate business, including a proposal to assist the past agency with their policies on a contract basis for their sale. Remarkably, the very next day, as if in response to my surrender, intense focus, and preparation, the floodgates of opportunity opened. New clients and contracts poured in at an astonishing rate, and it seemed like my business had taken off almost overnight. Within a month, my ex-boyfriend moved out, and I was well on my way to building a thriving coaching practice!

It's incredible to reflect on how much has unfolded over the past two decades. In those early years, I dedicated myself to mastering the art of networking. I distinctly remember coming across a book by Dr. Ivan Misner that presented a revealing statistic: on average, people are more likely to share dissatisfaction with 13 others, mention a positive experience to three, and remain silent if their expectations are met. This insight spurred me into action! I made a firm commitment from the outset to always strive to exceed expectations. Any other approach wouldn't have been a sustainable long-term strategy. As a result, I became skilled at understanding people's desires and needs. My business flourished primarily through referrals—by consistently going above and beyond expectations and having satisfied clients spread the word about the value of coaching. And to this day, it remains my top marketing strategy.

Furthermore, I continually reinvent my business and services to align with evolving customer needs. Every business contends with market shifts, industry disruptions, and technological advances. Consider the profound impact of the pandemic and the emergence of A.I. My primary focus is on anticipating how I can adapt my business to navigate these changes. I contemplate which topics will be most relevant, which platforms will be most suitable, and what unique contributions I can make. I position myself not just to identify opportunities but to seize them actively. For instance, I had already adopted Zoom for online coaching long before the pandemic necessitated it. I integrated technological platforms to streamline my business operations, allowing me to concentrate on coaching rather than administrative tasks. As my business expanded, so did my services. Initially, I coached business owners, given their prevalence in my networking circles. However, I later diversified to offer career coaching, particularly during economic downturns like the recession and the recent phenomenon of the great resignation. My passion for coaching teens led to an expansion of my services, as I recognized the potential for greater impact beyond the constraints of a social service agency. Executive coaching and leadership coaching hold immense influence, as the approach of leaders has ripple effects throughout organizations. My commitment to continuous learning and growth prompted me to return to school at the age of forty to complete my doctorate in human behavior. The more I learn, the better equipped I am to assist others. It's truly fulfilling when my clients express that they can approach me with any question, whether it's about parenting, health and wellness, or optimizing business profitability. My holistic approach is the cornerstone of my unique positioning in the coaching landscape.

THE IMPACT

I'm still not great with praise and compliments, but I consistently hear that I've changed people's lives. At first, I thought this was a bit dramatic, but now I can truly see how the work I do has an unbelievable ripple effect. It touches marriages, children, employees, and even the guy at the grocery store. When people become better versions of themselves, everyone benefits. That's my goal as a coach: to make a difference. I've had the opportunity to work with all kinds of people and businesses. I've helped businesses in various industries, including insurance, healthcare, legal, construction, real estate, trades, technology, banking, and more. I cherish the variety and the knowledge gained from understanding these diverse businesses. Initially, some people believed they should work with a coach who had a background in their specific field. However, I've come to realize that it's not about knowing the industry; it's about understanding people, and that is my specialty. One of my clients even affectionately nicknamed me the "People Whisperer" because of my ability to comprehend people and assist with change, motivation, communication, conflict resolution, focus, and performance.

These days, my work encompasses training, coaching (private, group, and team), and consulting. I place a significant focus on mindset and how shifting our mindset can expand our capacity. What I realized on that day when I felt devastated about being a failure was that I hadn't truly believed in myself. I had one foot out the door, contemplating whether I should seek another job, updating my resume, and searching. All of that took time away from my main mission: coaching people. Once I became fully committed to my mission, I gained the focus and motivation to persevere. When people overcome self-doubt and get out of their own way, the results they can achieve are astonishing!

Mindset permeates every aspect of our lives. It directs our focus and our actions. I've assisted clients in numerous areas, including hiring and firing decisions, succession planning, leadership development, productivity improvement, change management, conflict resolution, decision-making, and career exploration, among others. Each of these areas is tied to how individuals manage themselves and interact with others. People often spend a considerable amount of time puzzled by others' actions, trying to understand motivations, and seeking ways to motivate or eliminate drama. My coaching provides perspective and peace—intangible benefits that are truly priceless. Of course, people often achieve financial success, strengthen relationships, and expand their businesses as a result of my coaching. I've worked with numerous individuals who have become millionaires. However, what truly impresses me is the people they've become.

True wealth in life is about the quality of who you are and the impact you leave behind. That's what impresses me. Being a part of clients' lives as they graduate, get married, have children, achieve promotions, and navigate everything in between is incredibly satisfying. What makes me most proud is witnessing the lives my clients have created for themselves and becoming the individuals they've always aspired to be—whether it's being a better parent, a more effective leader, a supportive neighbor, a dedicated student, or simply a kinder human being. Being a part of this transformative journey is unparalleled, and it's the most rewarding experience I could ever ask for. I feel blessed to be a part of people's journeys, as they allow me into their lives and their hearts.

THE VISION

My vision is simple: to continue creating a ripple effect and coaching others to do the same. My formula is to be agile in discovering people's needs and generously give my gifts. This requires that I learn about others and about myself, and then I share it. I hesitate to share my formula because people often think they need to reproduce it. Instead, I encourage people to focus on their framework rather than the formula. A framework is how you approach your business based on your zone of genius. Discover who you are and what you have to contribute, then listen to what people truly need, and create services that combine both. Everyone's zone of genius is entirely different. While I do a lot of training and workshops, it's a great way to generate business, but beyond that, I love seeing the lightbulb moments. Many assume that they should also do training. However, if you don't have a passion for it, it will never be as successful as identifying those things that give you spark and make you shine. Your framework should be to determine those things for yourself.

Clearly, my strategy as an introvert needed to be different than if I were an extrovert. Next, determine your strategy for discovering people's needs, desires, and wants. I'm great at listening, so I continually collect information to learn about people, especially those in my target markets. The intersection between identifying needs and sharing my gifts is how I seize opportunities. It's how this all started when I had that first meeting with the business owner about my own business experience.

My vision is to continue fine-tuning this process. I firmly believe that coaching needs to be brought to the mainstream. It is so powerful that everyone should have this privilege; it shouldn't be reserved for those with money. So, I've spent years figuring out how to scale myself and duplicate my services. This journey led me to develop online coaching courses, with my signature program called B.O.U.N.C.E., designed to help people build resilience. My goal was to expand my programs to support teens in building resilience, but what I found was that the information was just as relevant for business owners and executives. So, I've worked diligently to create an online program at www.bounceclass. com and expand to cover many other topics. These courses are curated based on the topics that frequently come up with coaching clients and corporate training needs. This format provides a far more affordable and accessible avenue to professional growth. It's just one more step in my formula: identify needs and share generously.

As I reflect on this incredible journey, from battling imposter syndrome and addiction to transforming my life into one dedicated to helping others, I'm reminded of a valuable lesson I learned along the way: "God's delay is not God's denial." Life often throws us unexpected challenges and delays, but it's our determination and unwavering belief in our purpose that truly define our path. My vision is simple: to continue creating a ripple effect, coaching others to do the same, and bringing coaching to the mainstream so that everyone can benefit from its power. My journey is a testament to the power of resilience, determination, and the belief in oneself. I'm grateful for the opportunity to have been a part of so many people's transformative journeys, and I look forward to continuing to make a positive impact in the lives of others as we all move forward together.

Thank you for sharing in my story and may we all continue to strive for greatness and inspire those around us.

DR ROBIN LAVITCH, PCC, PhD, nicknamed "The People Whisperer", is the founder of Surpass Your Goals, a coaching practice for doctors, lawyers, entrepreneurs, executives, tweens, and more. Robin is an expert in helping clients and companies communicate with different personality styles, leverage their strengths, and integrate psychological insights for better results. Her coaching and training programs deliver shortcuts, formulas, and blueprints on being your best and figuring out what makes people tick. Her proven three-step process helps anyone overcome obstacles with insight, inspiration, and implementation. Her capacity to connect with audiences, elicit thought-provoking ideas and clarify personal ambitions prepares people to apply that knowledge instantaneously to accelerate their performance and productivity.

Website: www.surpassyourgoals.com
LinkedIn: https://www.linkedin.com/in/robinlavitch/

CAROLIN ZAMZOW

January 2019. After completing the seventh consecutive night shift, I drove home for about 25 minutes on the freeway, ready to collapse into bed. 48 hours later, the evening shift awaited me. So, with roughly 5 hours of sleep – as that's usually all I could manage – I had about 1.5 days of recovery before starting the new 7-day shift. That short period allowed me to get back on track, engage in some socializing, and do some exercise. Once a month, there was a long weekend to look forward to, but otherwise, it was a routine of functioning. Doing what was expected, week after week and month after month, because one had everything needed – financial security and perceived stability. Fulfillment? Hardly, at least not for someone wired like me.

Hi, I'm Caro, born in 1987, and I've decided to resign after 12 years of shift work as a chemical technician in a large company to pursue my dreams. I want to take you on a journey filled with inner struggles, uncertainties, doubts, opposing voices, and, ultimately, how I managed to turn my passion into a profession.

After graduating, I was aimless. I had no idea what career path to pursue. I sent out 2 job applications and received an offer for an apprenticeship as a chemical technician at a well-regarded local company. My parents were proud; it was a solid education with the prospect of a stable job. What more could one ask for? After completing the apprenticeship, I transitioned into a temporary position, which later turned into a permanent one after 2 years. The initial years were filled with learning, everything was new, and I was kept busy. After a few years, I received a salary increase based on my qualifications and also took on the role of on-site trainer, guiding apprentices during their practical assignments.

In 2014, my husband and I bought a house – a dream of mine. I enjoy being hands-on, creating our own little sanctuary. However, with the house came financial dependence. Initially, it didn't stress me much, knowing there was a certain income available each month.

At that time, my life revolved around three significant pillars that were important to me:

My life at that time revolved around three significant pillars: my relationship, my band, and, to be more specific, Powerlifting. This involves bringing one's maximum strength for a single repetition, ideally in competition, in squat, bench press, and deadlift, onto the platform. On weekends when I wasn't working or playing gigs with the band, we traveled to Berlin. We frequented a gym from its founding in 2014 – the Berlin Strength. It's not just any gym; it's rugged, devoid of frills, vegan, located on the RAW grounds in Berlin Friedrichshain, surrounded by alternative clubs and bars. We felt a strong connection to these people and the gym's attitude.

I trained 4-5 times a week, depending on how I could best integrate workouts into my shift schedule. It was a necessity, even if it meant going to the late shift feeling quite tired and exhausted. Before the shift or the day before, I prepared my meals for work as I didn't want to rely on cafeteria food. The sport provided me with physical fitness that benefitted my job. I could handle physical work without hesitation. Taking care of myself and being mindful of what I fed my body contributed to a sense of self-worth. I'll circle back later on the impact the sport had on the things that unfolded in the future.

Work had its good, bad, and not-so-bad days. Everyone can relate to that. What primarily challenged me was the rotating sleep schedule, few weekends off, and the work environment. The environment can significantly impact well-being at work. It makes a difference whether you're constantly dealing with people immersed in pessimism, blaming others for their own dissatisfaction, or if you're surrounded by thoughtful individuals who uplift you. Unfortunately, the former dominated. When conflicting worldviews collide without common ground for discussion, it can be truly draining.

Initially, I engaged in these discussions. Often, I found myself in tears in the restroom, unable to comprehend the level of hatred people could harbor. Today, I understand they were simply desperate, unwilling to admit their own responsibility for taking control of their lives. I also realized that my happiness couldn't depend on external factors, and I was responsible for how I reacted in that situation. It marked the shift from reactive to proactive behavior.

In 2019, I applied for part-time work. Financially, we were doing well, and the idea of having two extra free days didn't take much consideration. Fortunately, the request was approved. In hindsight, this marked the first confrontation with a growing aversion to work and a desire for more leisure time. Simultaneously, there was a certain lack of understanding about why I would choose to work part-time. After all, I was young, without kids, and supposedly had no other commitments.

I discovered that those who complained the loudest were often the ones who, due to their own dissatisfaction, had lost sight of possible changes to pursue contentment. Resignation on every level. Sure, I had less money due to the reduction in hours. Was it worth it? Absolutely YES! It was my decision, and it felt good.

2020: the year of the pandemic and, for me, a year of transformation. The intervals during which I reflected on my current situation and questioned whether I truly wanted to stick with this job until retirement decreased, and the desire for change grew because the answer increasingly became NO. Weighing whether to continue on the safe path or embark on a challenging one, marked by uncertainty about whether this path would even lead to the desired destination, is the greatest challenge our minds can present. Our brains are wired for safety and equilibrium. Uncertainty signifies imbalance, danger. Thoughts can render you paralyzed. Thoughts aim to keep you safe. However, we can view thoughts as an opportunity, learn to accept and interpret them. A thought can grow, along with the impulse to take action. Recognizing this, we become aware that we have the power to change things within our sphere of influence.

So, I had to make a change, and I knew only I could kick-start it. I believe many people are unhappy in their jobs or current life situations, but very few actually change anything because it requires effort. It means leaving the benevolent comfort zone repeatedly. After the first minor setback, one tends to crawl back into the safety zone. It's familiar, tried and tested. The body and the brain are highly energy-conscious systems. Our thoughts literally have us in their grip.

I didn't want to be the person who eventually says, 'I wish I had...' Often, we wait for the right moment to tackle things. Yet, this waiting is precisely another mechanism trying to prevent us from breaking free, breaking out of the comfort zone. Things rarely change so drastically that one encounters the "perfect" moment to make decisions and initiate changes. Nothing will happen on its own, except for the years passing by and the 'I wish I had' growing larger.

I had two options: applying elsewhere, possibly ending up in the same unfulfilling spiral after a few years, or daring to venture into something completely new and more fulfilling.

The former would have been the easier path, but doubts crept in at the thought of similar work. As mentioned earlier, sports played and continue to play a crucial role in my life. I've always been active, participating in various team sports during childhood and adolescence. In 2007, at the age of 19, I discovered strength training through my husband, and we supported each other in competitions.

During that time, I tried many approaches to become more muscular, defined, and, of course, to compete in my weight class under 57kg. One is conditioned to choose the easiest path and falsely believes there are shortcuts. When the desired results didn't materialize after a few weeks, disappointment followed. I experimented with various dietary approaches. In hindsight, I wasted years where I left a lot of potential on the table. Seeking help was not an option because I was ambitious enough to keep trying on my own. In retrospect, more wasted years. We often think we have to handle everything ourselves. A misconception. Seeking help, coaching from experts who have been through it, who know the ropes, puts you on the fast track. Investing in the development of your own skills reveals the power of your own actions.

So, it had to be something related to sports. The idea of being able to provide personal training filled me with a lot of joy. I scoured the internet for possible training options alongside my job and began self-studying to become a fitness trainer. Going through the material was easy because it interested me, and I had a vision. The imagination of my 'future self' gave me so much strength to pursue this path. We underestimate how much our imagination can influence our decisions and sharpen our focus on the things that are necessary. Directing our attention to the positive, rather than following thoughts that repeatedly try to divert our energy.

For the first time, I enlisted the help of a coach, a bodybuilding coach. Firstly, to try something different after 12 years of powerlifting, and secondly, to free up mental capacity by not having to think about my own training. I had a professional I trusted, so I just had to execute.

I also learned a lot about online coaching – the process, where to focus, training design, mental work. Learning from the best provided me with confidence. Even though I wasn't coaching anyone at that time, I created forms, templates, guidelines. I wanted to be prepared, just like in sports, just like with my pre-prepared meals.

I lean a bit towards perfectionism, which can be hindering as it makes one get lost in details, thinking that it won't work otherwise. Then you see the whole mountain of work, everything that still needs to be prepared, and you start feeling desperate. It can render you almost incapable of action because you're not focusing on the individual step but only see this enormous hole that needs filling. It's a killer when it comes to efficiency and progress. It's those many small steps that set the stone in motion.

I successfully completed my training as a fitness trainer, continually expanding my knowledge on the side by attending seminars and reading books. Everything revolved around it. Work, on the other hand, became secondary, devoid of emotions. I was doing only what was necessary.

Two friends of mine wanted to start weight training. They had already signed up at the gym. After a brief equipment introduction, they received an uninspiring training plan. Sound familiar? They asked me for help, knowing I had several years of experience in strength training. We scheduled a few training sessions. Man, that was an amazing feeling. Finally, I could share my knowledge and gain practical experience with people.

My path was clear — I wanted exactly that, desperately! I started showcasing the progress of my friends and my knowledge on social media. I needed a platform to gain practical experience and, through recommendations, develop a following.

With my part-time job, I now had a few extra days to work at a gym on the side. I took the initiative and applied for a part-time job at Berlin Strength. After a few weeks – an acceptance.

That was the point where everything changed abruptly. My enthusiasm was unstoppable. I tried to be on-site as often as possible. I should mention that I live about 1.5 hours away. But it was worth it to me. I used the time on the train, for example, to continue my education. Personal training inquiries started coming in through the gym. With the team's approval, I was allowed to conduct my first training session. I was so nervous. I had been agonizing over what to do for days, and, of course, everything turned out differently. The classic. I felt really uncomfortable on-site, but I tried not to show my uncertainty to give the person a sense of security. This event was groundbreaking, and I knew the more I faced these situations, the more my real confidence would grow. People aren't machines where we can plan something in advance; we have to act situationally based on our experience.

The more time I spent in the gym, the less motivation I had to be active in my main job. The thought of having to go on shifts saddened me. I now had this direct comparison of what "work" could mean. At the same time, it was an extreme double burden, demanding a lot from me, and other leisure activities took a back seat. Certainly, it was also a strain on my relationship. However, I never felt that my partner didn't support me during this time, and I'm very grateful for that. We talked a lot, and I expressed my doubts and fears about quitting such a well-paying job and having to live with much less, an amount that wouldn't even cover the mortgage on our house. But I simply couldn't work there anymore. If my fears had prevailed, I think I would have become very, very unhappy. And I had seen more than enough of what can arise from dissatisfaction.

We scheduled a meeting with the gym team. I explained my current situation. I calculated a thousand times how much money I would need to get by. They shared their own experiences and mentioned that it would take about six months until I could earn a decent income with additional coaching. Opting for a part-time job meant being socially insured, a significant benefit. After our meeting, I took a few days to go through everything again, for the thousandth time, to analyze and calculate.

In the meantime, I had also applied for another part-time job as a fitness trainer at a newly established gym in the region. However, I received a rejection. No matter how many times I crunched the numbers, it always came out the same. These figures scared me. So, it was a matter of weighing the options again. Only this time, I didn't give negativity any space and focused on what lay ahead.

On January 28, 2021, I submitted my resignation. My mother, my grandmother, they were bewildered. How could I? Out of security, into uncertainty. This was the final step, and it felt damn good. I felt an inner relief for having done what my gut feeling had been trying to convey to me for months. Everything improved instantly. I only had one month left to endure. Of course, these days, I occasionally think back to that time because it was very influential and lengthy. Pursuing that job provided me with many opportunities but didn't fulfill me. An important factor when it comes to personal happiness.

I knew it was really starting now. I was responsible for building my own business to strengthen my financial independence alongside the low income from the gym. Taking proactive action instead of waiting to see what happens.

What does training have to do with it?

Training is one of the best investments. It can provide a powerful input when it comes to nutrition, well-being, and daily structure. Engage with nutrition, engage with yourself. It becomes a self-runner.

Training forces you to plan more. You become more efficient, more reflective. You take care of yourself and yet remain more flexible with your nutrition. It establishes habits. You are the mirror image of your habits. Training is an investment that doesn't pay off immediately but unfolds its full power through momentum. The same can be applied to a budding business. If you have stamina and don't give up, even when the multitude of work seemingly generates no output, it is precisely that work that makes you grow. Setbacks, making mistakes, mean growth. Of course, we shouldn't blindly start a project with unbridled optimism, thinking everything will work out. The healthy middle ground, taking a risk while knowing there will be setbacks, defines expectations and how we ultimately deal with mistakes. Whether we draw strength from them or despair and resign.

Without Berlin Strength, without this platform, without gaining the necessary practical experience, without this community, it would have definitely unfolded differently.

At the moment, I coach around 30 people, sometimes more, sometimes fewer, and within a quarter of a year, I've been able to establish a solid financial foundation. As mentioned earlier, humans are not machines. Empathy, emotionality, trust are the things that provide me with tremendous added value in my work.

Seeing how they unfold their own potential, surpass themselves, and hold onto things even when obstacles arise. Believing in themselves and seeing setbacks as opportunities instead of throwing in the towel and convincing themselves they're not good enough. Reflecting on themselves and seeing each day as a new opportunity to grow. Not just physically but also mentally. That drives me. I can be who I am. I can strengthen my own strengths and recognize and work on my mental weaknesses. Because our own greatest opponent is ourselves.

CAROLIN ZAMZOW is a certified coach and seminar instructor who helps women strengthen their self-confidence, work on their body composition, and achieve their ideal figure through strength training and goal-oriented nutrition. Her coaching is personal, empathetic, and aims to overcome personal barriers and beliefs to become a better version of oneself. As a team member of Berlin Strength, she assists numerous people in achieving these goals both in person and online.

Website: *https://www.cz-coaching.de*
Instagram: *https://www.instagram.com/caro_berlinstrength*

GAELLE CHATENET

My first encounter with sophrology was during a stay in France, my home country, over the summer 2010. Earlier that year I had given birth to my first child in my adoptive country, Japan. Giving birth so far away from home and my family would not have been easy in any case, but it was made even harder by a car accident that happened 10 days before my scheduled delivery date. Heavily pregnant, I got in my friend's car to go into central Tokyo and meet our former colleagues for a baby shower lunch together. Unfortunately, we didn't make it as a truck driver drove through a stop sign without stopping, bumped into a car that, in turn, bumped into my friend's car, sending us into a concrete wall. The whole left side of the car hit the wall. People drive on the left side of the road in Japan. So the driver is on the right. Thankfully, my friend's 2-year-old was safely in his car seat behind his Mom. I was the only one sitting on the left side of the car. My left knee, thigh, elbow and the left part of my forehead hit the side of the car and the wall. I have no recollection of that day after we left from the parking lot where we met at 11 AM until after 5PM. I was conscious the whole time but because of the shock, I had no short time memory for several hours. I only remember asking my husband where I was, around 5PM, and seeing the surprise in his eyes when he realized I was finally 'back'.

This was also the start of a long process with hospitals and insurance companies. Lots of appointments, stress and questions.

Two weeks later I gave birth. The birth of a first child is always a complicated situation. Mine was made harder by the fact that I had, among other wounds, a broken knee which not only interfered with the delivery itself but also the first few weeks of life, alone with a new born and unable to walk properly. It was a busy, exhausting time and days and nights seemed to bleed into each other. My husband had just started a job at a new Japanese company and was always traveling and working later.

On a regular check up with my doctor I mentioned to him that I had developed a fear of death that was so strong it was almost incapacitating. I couldn't watch the news because anything I saw I thought would happen to me, I was convinced of my imminent death and that I would leave my child motherless. In the few hours when I could actually sleep, the fear would often keep me awake.

The doctor told me I was having Post Partum Depression. This was very surprising to me as I was not feeling depressed but he told me this was actually a symptom. I was not keen on medication as I was breastfeeding and don't like medication that alters the mood in general. He gave me some very light ones that made me feel good enough to function. When I went to France that summer, I accompanied my Mom to her Sophrology class and the effect and relief were so good I almost fell asleep right there. I asked her teacher to see me for a private session. After a few sessions I could see a huge change in how I was feeling. She gave me a series of exercises and directions to follow so that I could continue on my own once I was back in Japan.

I always reverted back to the exercises when I felt stress after that. I didn't study Sophrology farther at the time but always read the periodic emails she sent and tried the exercises she offered in them. A few years later my son who was 8 started having a school phobia and developed several OCD behaviors. It was so hard to see him suffer and his mood swings, erratic behavior and episodic fits of crying were not only awful to witness, they disrupted the whole family. I feared for him, for his little brother, and for our family as a whole. I took him to the same sophrologist over the summer break and she helped him so much, I asked her to teach me a few exercises I could help him do. When I got back to Japan I signed up for an online training to be a sophrologist so I could help him as much as possible. It took one year and a half to complete the training. Having done that, I could help him more and I also started helping some friends or their children, just informally when we met. The idea of doing this professionally crossed my mind several times but it just never seemed to be the right time.

Later on, I decided to take a coaching training, with the same school in France where I had studied Sophrology. Our first coaching assignment was a self-analysis and at one thing I had mentioned, my teacher wrote a note in the margin 'Maybe NLP could help?'. I had no idea what NLP was. I googled it and read all the articles I could find and was so intrigued and wanted to know more. I ordered a book online and read through it and was even more curious to learn and know more. I signed up with the NLP comprehensive institute in the US and started studying

NLP as well.

So, there I was, certified Sophrologist, Coach and NLP practitioner, working as an admin in an international school.

I often thought about starting a practice but it was such a big jump from where I was. I had a very nice job, lovely colleagues, a lovely boss, a family that relied on me… Why change everything and jump into the unknown? What if I did and then regretted it? What if I started a practice and it didn't work out? So many questions and so much fear, and yet the idea kept coming back every now and then… And then, COVID happened… Such an unprecedented crisis. No-one saw it coming and we all had to adapt quickly and as best we could. The school I was working at being an international school, most students were foreigners. During he first year of COVID, not much changed, as all the expats stayed in Tokyo as the whole world seemed to come to a halt. The second year, the people who were scheduled to take different positions abroad all left, but Japan had closed its borders so no one could come in and all the international schools' enrollments dropped drastically as a consequence. There were long talks in the office, discussing how to best save the school but also keep the staff where possible... Reducing the number of workdays and hours, changing roles…

It was in that moment that I realized that this terrible, terrible time was actually giving me a great opportunity. There was truly no need for me to stay for the school as two persons would be plenty to run the office given the number of students. And while part of me wanted to stay in the safety of my position, another part got really excited and thought

'This is my time! This is the sign I have been waiting for! It is time for me to jump and try something new!'. And so, I did!

It was really a jump into the unknown as I had no idea how to open a practice in Japan, advertise for it, get clients…

There is an association for French Women in Tokyo called FAJ (Facilitating Women's Ambition in Japan) and part of their many actions is a 9 months program for women entrepreneurs who wish to start a business in Japan. While the program is nearly free, you need to apply and present your project to the persons in charge and they are the one who decide whether or not you can join the group. I nervously drew a draft of my project and was lucky to be able to join, together with 10 other women. We all had different projects, artists, web designers, yoga instructors, in-company training professionals…All different but all equally motivated and passionate about our projects. Under the supervision of two super-women, we attended monthly meetings, each one designed to show us one side of business that we would then have to work on. The synergy of the group was so important and a huge part in the success of my project. As all entrepreneurs know, there are so many ups and downs. It is so easy to go from euphoria to despair and having this group of women as a constant support was the key to navigating the moments of self-doubt and concern.

The biggest challenge for me was the creation of my website, which I ended up doing by myself over the course of a month. I was given the advice that creating it myself would give me full control over it, I would be able to make changes anytime myself and really be able to create exactly what I wanted. For a super low-tech person like me (I still use a paper diary that I carry everywhere in my purse and gets me so many interesting comments each time…) it was much easier said than done but eventually I did it and when I had nearly finished it, I deleted it all! The reason was that, while I liked the contents, I was unhappy with the lay out. So, I deleted and redid it, this time to my liking, within two days. Except for the two persons I asked to check for spelling mistakes and other corrections, I didn't tell anyone for a few days. Just knowing that my site existed and that people could find and read it was both a huge thrill and so scary at first. I am not a social media person, I am very secretive about so many aspects of my life, sharing so much information on a website for all to see really felt like a huge jump into the unknown. But finally, I did!

First, I shared it with friends and got really good return. Then I worked on the SEO and I started getting traffic. I advertised in Facebook groups, left name cards wherever foreigners might be in Tokyo, and tried to promote as much as possible. Again, when you are like me, quite secretive about your life and not used to talking about yourself, it is not easy to go out into the world and start telling people about what you do. But it became easier and easier as time went by.

And finally, the day came when someone contacted me to schedule a session. It was so thrilling! I had done this on myself, my son, my friends before, I had full confidence in the process and the method, and yet, upon receiving that first inquiry I was filled with doubt and fear. What if for some reason it didn't work? What if the person didn't like me? All of a sudden there were so many things that came to mind that I had never thought about before. Also, one thing that surprised me is that the first person to contact me was a man. While I am happy to work with all genders, I felt surprised that my website which is so feminine would appeal to a man. Yes, I really asked myself every possible question!

So, the big day came and… he was late! I was so nervous! I thought he wasn't coming… I felt bad and defeated and anxious… and suddenly, a knock on the door! He was just lost on the way to my house which isn't surprising in the tiny streets of Tokyo. We had our first session and it was great. As were all first sessions after that. Later I realized a really important thing about my website and the importance of creating a site that looks and feels like you. Because when people go through my website, they already know the kind of person I am, they get to feel what it will be like to work with me and whether we are suitable for each other or not. What I came to realize if that, if they like what they see, then we're going to get along and work well together. What I had only considered as a way to get people to know about my practice turned out to be a great introduction.

And slowly, I started to get more clients, more requests. My practice is located near the French school in Tokyo, so I also get to help middle and high school students who are having a hard time getting used to life in Japan or who are stressed for their exams, as well as some who encounter more serious issues like bullying, school phobia or anorexia.

I work with both children (from 7 year old and up) and adults. Men and Women. French or English speakers. What I love is the connection I create with each one of my patients. I care about each one of them and

I love the trust they put in me. I love to see them progress, reach their goals, change their lives. It gives me the feeling that I am doing some good in this crazy world we live in, at my own level. I believe in the connection between all people and that doing good for one person always has positive repercussions, not only for that person but also for the people they will interact with. I receive so many positive comments. I love the smile on my patients faces when they leave after a session. I love watching the changes in the physiognomy from the time they enter to the time we finish working together. Sometimes we do exercises that are really structures, and sometimes much more subtle and they will tell me things like 'We didn't really work that much today, but I really feel much better/lighter/happier'. I just smiled and assure them that we did work, but work on the mind doesn't always have to be fully conscious.

It's been two years now since my first patient came to knock on the door and I have seen so many people and heard so many life stories. I have seen so many tears but also many smiles. I don't think I could go back to doing anything else now that I have tasted the freedom of working for myself and the satisfaction of helping people. It is a very nourishing sensation and I sometimes feel like they are doing as much good to me as I do to them. I learn from each one, each conversation. I recognize parts of myself in each one of them.

I feel so lucky to be able to work in something I love so much.

I went back to France for the summer last year and everyone I know told me I look great, so happy, fulfilled and even younger! How could I not when my life has changed in such a drastic and wonderful way? While I loved my past job, this opportunity as given me so much to be grateful for.

I can feel that it changed me as well. I met so many wonderful people, I have become more open and relaxed and happy. People are always drawn to happiness and there is so much positivity in my life.

Sophrology and NLP help me every day to become more and more the person I want to be, to live my life to the fullest and to bring good around me. I found my wellbeing and sharing it with others makes it even more powerful.

I have private sessions as well as couple therapy sessions where both partners attend together. It is always great to see love, trying to make it through and I feel really grateful for the trust my patients put in me.

I have started running workshops in international communities around Tokyo.

While one on one sessions are great, I also enjoy the atmosphere and the synergy of the groups. Again, I come to 'teach' at these workshops but I end up learning so much myself, every single time! It is amazing.

My hope is that I can keep on growing my practice, keep on meeting new people and help them, learn from them. The human mind is infinite and there is always more to learn. The more people are at peace with who they are and accepting of themselves, the more balanced the world will be. To anyone thinking about starting a business, I would say: take that jump! And the question I ask all of my patients when they are faced with a decision: Think about it, really think about it: what is the worst that could happen?

I once had a patient who refused to answer this question. He was scared of losing his job if he did something and I challenged him with the question: what is the worst that could happen if you lost that job? He could just not even consider the possibility. So, I let it go. It was just too much to ask of him at that time. At the next session he came back and told me he had thought about it and yes, there would definitely be difficulties involved in the potential loss of his job, but eventually things would settle, and he would find another one and all in all, while there would definitely be negatives, there would also be positives. And the more he thought about it, the less serious the negatives became. Mistakes will happen, trouble and inconveniences, but when you look at all the good left, as long as you are still here, still alive, you can pick yourself up and start building again. At the end of your story, what you will remember the most are all the unplanned moments, running in the rain when you forgot your umbrella, the epic fails you made it through. Don't limit yourself, don't let fear scare you away from living your best life. It is yours and it is now, make the most of it!

GAELLE CHATNET is is a French citizen who has been residing in Tokyo, Japan for the last 20 years. Though she has a business background, a car accident in 2010 and the subsequent recovery process introduced her to Sophrology and NLP. This experience eventually led her to switch careers completely, and what had been one of the worst moments in her life ended up changing it for the better. She launched her coaching and well-being business two years ago.

Website: *https://www.sophrologyandcoachintokyo.com/*

VICO MADRID

MY STORY, WHERE I STARTED.

Pinpointing the exact inception of my entrepreneurial journey isn't straightforward. The desire existed since 2015, yet the path wasn't immediately clear. Gradually, I embarked on a process of information gathering, gaining experience, pursuing a second degree in business, obtaining a yoga teaching certification, living in diverse countries, and seeking therapy. Every challenge became an opportunity, solidifying my commitment to inch closer to realizing my dream.

My initial plan to relocate from the UK to Denmark, while initially perceived as a 'failure,' led me to something even better. Living in Edinburgh for three years with the goal of refining my English, I simultaneously worked with individuals facing learning difficulties, leveraging my first degree in Occupational Therapy. My intention was to prepare for the IELTS exam to pursue a Master's in Public Health in Denmark, aiming to elevate my career. Despite passing the exam, I faced rejection for the Master's program, a moment of profound disappointment. Yet, in embracing this setback, a new opportunity emerged. During this acceptance process, a conversation with a good friend who once shared a flat with me played a pivotal role.

V: I feel that the months studying for that exam were a waste of time. What am I going to do now in Denmark!?! I made up my mind to move there already.

N: Vico, maybe life is telling you that it is time to do something that you really want to do.

V: What do you mean?

N: Well, I saw how much you enjoy doing yoga along with the rehabilitation of your ankle. Why don't you get a certification to be a yoga teacher?

V: What?!?! You are joking right?! I can't even touch my toes!!!

N: You know very well that you don't need to touch your toes to be a good teacher. The most important thing is that you find passion for what you are teaching and I can see how much you enjoy yoga. Also you could start your career as a yoga teacher in Denmark, why not?

V: Yes, well, maybe you have a point. I will think about it

After leaving the kitchen, a curiosity-driven search for yoga teacher certifications in Copenhagen led me to enroll in a course just a week later. This marked the beginning of my yoga teacher career and set the stage for my entrepreneurial journey.

I relocated to Denmark in July 2018, completing my yoga teacher certification by November. Equipped and eager, I initiated my teaching journey with classes in my brother's gym in Spain and a nursing home working with individuals in wheelchairs. This experience proved eye-opening, establishing a connection between my two worlds: Occupational Therapy and yoga.

Initiating my yoga career in Denmark, I taught classes in various studios and simultaneously embarked on branding Yoga with Vico. In tandem, I sought therapy to address and overcome my limiting beliefs—a universal challenge we all face. A significant hurdle for me was grappling with the pervasive thought: 'I am not good enough.'

As I observed the challenges of establishing a full-time career as a yoga teacher, I sought additional employment to sustain myself, a situation many yoga teachers face (details explored later in this chapter). Through a fortuitous encounter at a business school open house, I discovered that the IELTS English exam, initially taken for my Master's application, could be applied towards enrolling in the AP Degree of Marketing Management. The effort invested in that exam unexpectedly opened doors, aligning with my vision of opening my own company, leading to approval in the Marketing Management program.

The notion of a 'right moment' to start a business is elusive; doubts persist, but external factors can present solutions to new problems. In my case, the onset of Covid-19 prompted a shift. Recognizing the strain on mental and emotional health, I pivoted my yoga courses online, requiring flexibility and adaptability to the 'new normal,' ensuring the quality of my offerings in the online modality.

Many NEW SKILLS were learned

How to live stream with good quality sound and image.

Being able to have the right frame and lighting in the living so my students could follow the classes the best.

Give online guidance with the classes that will not require physical adjustments of my students.

Undoubtedly, transitioning online posed its challenges. Each time I went online, the fear of potential connection issues lurked (a familiar experience when stepping out of the comfort zone).

Recognizing the swift rise of online yoga, a manifestation of market traction, I saw an opportunity to establish my brand. Leveraging my network, I reached out to a professional graphic designer friend, initiating a six-week collaboration to design my logo. Using the income from my online teaching, I paid her. Our weekly meetings, fueled by my clear vision, led us through the admirable process of exploring various drafts until we found 'the one.' Surprisingly time-consuming, yet the outcome endures, as I continue to proudly display the same logo today.

Transforming challenges into opportunities is a core strength that bolsters my resilience. During the uncertainty and stress of the Covid-19 era, I crafted a unique online course integrating yoga, breathing exercises, meditation, and journaling—a resounding success with participants worldwide.

Simultaneously, while developing my logo, I launched my Instagram and Facebook pages, sharing my yoga story. A year later, I invested in my first website with the help of a web developer.

Reflecting on 2015, the year I first envisioned opening my own company, let me delve into that story. My initial job as a graduate in Occupational Therapy at a nursing home prompted contemplation about my professional journey. Despite my dedication to impactful rehabilitation programs, the less-than-ideal working conditions and leadership concerns led me to question: 'Is it all?'

As a big dreamer, my desire to master my English in an English-speaking country led me to pursue growth beyond the working conditions I had. Opting for professional expansion, I made a bold decision. With just three weeks' notice, I condensed my life into two suitcases, leaving behind summer clothes and embarking on a one-way journey to Edinburgh.

MY FAMILY BACKGROUND
AN IMPORTANT PIECE OF ME

Born into a hard-working family in the quaint town of Argamasilla de Alba, nestled in the heart of Castilla-La Mancha, known for Don Quixote, windmills, and castles, I am the eldest of three siblings.

My father, opening a construction company when I was just 5 years old, provided me with an early glimpse into the world of entrepreneurship, influencing my positive stance toward starting my own venture. Though he never directly suggested it, his example spoke volumes. My parents instilled in me essential values, emphasizing the importance of hard work and the understanding that money doesn't grow on trees. From the age of 16 to 21, I worked each summer to save for university and travels. My dad's advice, 'When you have an education, you can choose between a qualified and a non-qualified job,' resonated deeply, underscoring their commitment to providing educational opportunities they couldn't have. Observing my dad navigate the intricacies of his company taught me valuable lessons, and I'm grateful for the dedication he put into ensuring the best possible education. Even as a teenager, I played a role, managing invoices when they invested in their first desktop computer.

DOUBTS AND CHALLENGES

Several years into my life in Denmark, a formidable challenge emerged when my dad was diagnosed with cancer, and its rapid progression demanded a return to Spain to support him and my family. His sudden passing hit me profoundly, prompting the decision to seek help from a psychologist. This marked the beginning of my therapy journey—an action long contemplated but finally initiated in the wake of this life-altering event.

Over the years, I've witnessed the positive impact on both my personal and professional life. A therapist with a holistic-integrative and somatic-trauma approach played a crucial role. Together, we addressed and replaced limiting beliefs, such as 'As an entrepreneur, I can't have free time.' Therapy became a tool to fortify my self-esteem and embrace my background. Connecting with my inner child, a deeply rewarding experience, later inspired the creation of a yoga course focused on the reconnection with the inner child. I strongly recommend therapy for everyone, especially entrepreneurs. You don't need to wait for a dramatic event to seek support; therapy is beneficial for personal growth and is the best investment you can make in yourself. Another notable challenge I faced was pursuing an AP degree in Marketing Management in English. I label it as a challenge for three reasons:

My background was in Health Sciences, therefore since high school I didn't study anything related to economics or business

The education was in English.

I did a student exchange, yes Erasmus with 28 (never too late) in a University in Finland

Reflecting on my time at the University of Applied Sciences of Haaga Helia, I am grateful for the opportunity to participate in courses not offered in Denmark, particularly in human resources and entrepreneurship. One standout experience was a project with Tespack, a high-tech company, during my studies in Marketing Management. My team and I undertook the challenge of developing an internationalization program for their innovative product—the solar backpack. Over the four months, I not only applied theoretical knowledge but also gained insights into real-life scenarios, particularly in negotiations. This experience underscored the importance of understanding one's value, the value of services, and addressing the needs while providing solutions.

I want to emphasize the importance of possessing the knowledge to create a **SUSTAINABLE** business and a **SOLID STRUCTURE**. It is crucial to diversify income sources by putting your eggs in several baskets (income flow from various sources). In my case, my company is entirely self-funded and has been growing organically since its inception.

You need to identify the solutions you are offering and, most importantly, to whom (considering the customer journey). Additionally, understanding external market factors, including macro and microeconomics, is crucial for long-term success. It's a fact that most startups fail within the first two years.

I personally struggled with setting prices for my services in the beginning, especially with a personal brand like mine. I found listing parameters such as development time, staff costs, and course expenses helpful. However, the key, in my experience, is to add value to what you offer. This helps carve a niche in the market, differentiating from the competition. The decision to study a business degree in the Nordics stemmed from a desire to move away from the Spanish educational system, which prioritizes memorization over practical application. I was drawn to the Nordic way of learning, which equips students to apply knowledge to real-world business issues. It provided a stark contrast to the memorization-focused approach in Spain where tests often had only one right answer. Studying in the Nordics instilled in me the ability to think independently and solve real problems. Companies would present cases at our business school, and we, in teams, had hours to devise solutions and present them to the CEO.

MY INTERSHIP AND THESIS

While teaching my first yoga classes, I faced the decision of where to do my internship. Motivated by a desire to delve deeper into the wellness industry, I chose a startup meditation app. This turned out to be one of the best decisions, as it allowed me to absorb knowledge about the startup ecosystem, providing valuable insights into how it relates to the business model I was developing behind the scenes.

Full-time yoga teachers in yoga studios operate as freelancers, invoicing each studio with an agreed-upon salary per class.

It's a common challenge that yoga teachers face, as they often engage in additional tasks beyond teaching without additional compensation. To achieve a decent salary, many teachers end up teaching numerous classes across different studios, dealing with commuting time. This scenario highlights the financial strain where teachers might need to conduct around 15-20 classes per week just to cover their expenses.

It's unfortunate but common for yoga teachers to face burnout within 1-2 years due to the physical and energetic demands. Many end up taking on a full-time job and teach only a few classes as a hobby. To avoid this path, I explored ways to solve the problem and build a sustainable career in an industry projected to reach $215 billion by 2025, which is currently valued at $105.9 billion.

Returning to my internship, I applied various models and gained crucial industry knowledge, especially from working with meditation teachers. I leveraged this experience for my thesis, outlining my BUSINESS MODEL's evolution from B2C to B2B in 2021. The challenge of writing the thesis became an opportunity to deeply understand the yoga market and create a distinctive business model. Currently, I'm focused on expanding further into the B2B space to make a more significant impact.

THE KEY OF ASKING FOR HELP

Seek for help, shake up your network!

Having a business mentor/coach can be invaluable in your journey. I was fortunate to find mine somewhat randomly in my Danish classes. It's an investment that pays off, offering reminders about crucial aspects, like celebrating milestones. My mentor, alongside my psychologist, played a pivotal role in building the confidence needed for setting prices. Despite having the theoretical knowledge of pricing strategies, doubts were abundant. With a clear vision of offering high-quality services, my mentor's guidance helped align the pricing accordingly.

Also another important part that I didn't learn was negotiation skills.

And once more I come back to the crucial aspect of therapy. A simple way how I saw one of the limiting beliefs I had (and still have) is the one of: 'I am not worthy/good enough' and this can reflect in your prices.

KNOW YOUR WORTH & BE READY TO SAY NO

With experience, you come to realize that not everyone is willing to pay your perceived value. In the early stages of my journey, a large company approached me to provide services for their members. They sought a unique and exclusive product involving the creation of a series of yoga videos, benefiting their 120,000 members across eleven countries. This collaboration became a valuable addition to the product they offer to their members. After a successful online meeting with the CEO, I crafted a prototype for the product, initiating negotiations. However, the discussion shifted to emails, handled by the project manager responsible for external partnerships. We had multiple online meetings where I presented the prototype, adjusting the proposal based on their feedback. Seeking guidance on budgeting for this new endeavor, I consulted both my accountant and business mentor. Balancing the desire not to lose the project while ensuring fair compensation for my value, we factored in considerations like copyrights and video distribution, elements I hadn't previously priced. Unfortunately, the company's response was; 'It is too expensive; we have someone with X followers in London who can do it for half the price.'

Honestly, it was a bummer; contemplating a reduction in the quality of my offering left me questioning, 'Would it have been worth it?' After taking a few days to reflect and calculating the hours required for the project, my gut feeling told me that compromising on payment would diminish my enjoyment in executing the work. Despite promises of exposure to 120,000 users, they insisted on paying 'half of my value,' framing it as an investment.

In the end, I said NO, and I don't regret it.

I've learned that exposure alone doesn't pay the bills. If a project isn't enjoyable for me, I won't get involved; work needs to be fun. My key takeaways include:

Listen more to their needs than providing solutions.

Ask all the questions.

Be sure that you are in communication with the person who is going to approve (or not) your budget.

Negotiations skills are not taught at university.

Cultural differences matter, in particular with online communication.

Calculating all project costs involves considering hidden expenses, such as time spent on email communication and video editing, in addition to direct expenses.

Be ready to stand firm on your feet about your offerings.

Price reflects value. Focus on adding more value.

WHO I HAVE BECOME
A FUTURE YET TO COME

My evolution has reached many different levels, and I know that I am only scratching the surface of the iceberg in terms of what the future holds. I initiated my company's branding in 2020, then transitioned to part-time work until February 2021 when I became a full-time member Currently, I am assembling a team of individuals to help me positively impact more lives and establish an organic business model focused on developing Health and Wellbeing programs for implementation in workplaces, fostering a better work-life balance. While my primary business model is B2B, I also engage in some B2C activities, such as teaching a few classes in a selected studio in Copenhagen, as part of my company's branding strategy. Additionally, I offer yoga retreats for B2C clients, and I am planning to introduce corporate retreats in the near future. Moreover, I organize events in collaboration with exceptional professionals, contributing to the success of my community, with many events selling out in 2023.

The knowledge I acquired through my business education has proven invaluable for my current endeavors. Having managed various interns, we're currently in the process of forming a stable team of three, presenting new leadership challenges. I'm focusing on honing my leadership skills to inspire and equip my team for success. Gratitude extends to those I've encountered on my journey, as each experience has contributed to my growth. Rooted in self-awareness, I'm crafting a work-life balance that aligns with my values. This pursuit of freedom mirrors the responsibility that comes with owning a company.

VICO MADRID graduated in 2014 with a BA in Occupational Therapy from the University of Castilla-la Mancha, in Spain. Since then, Vico has created health programs for individuals and groups, who suffers from different conditions, to make their lives more functional and independent. She created these programs for people, who were diagnosed with: Alzheimers, Parkinsons, brain damage, Down syndrome, amongst other mental health conditions, such as Bipolar Disorder, Schizophrenia, depression and anxiety. Vico founded *Yoga with Vico* in 2018, with the vision of using her wide knowledge in healthcare with focus on promoting people's well-being and build the best version of themselves, regarding in which condition they are at.

Website:	*https://yogawithvico.com/*
Instagram:	*https://www.instagram.com/yogawithvico/*
Facebook:	*https://www.facebook.com/yogawithvico*
LinkedIn:	*https://www.linkedin.com/in/vicomadrid/*

GINA UHRMEISTER

A TALE OF MISSING GLITTER, SOUL CONNECTION, AND THE WILD JOURNEY OF ENTREPRENEUERSHIP

Imagining and creating have always been part of my life's journey, so I decided to weave them into my professional path. The story really kicks off shortly after I finished my training.

My first job interview led me to a buzzing workplace where colleagues hurried between desks and the production hall with order folders in hand. Amidst this, a young woman with long black hair and a red-and-white polka-dot skirt caught my eye. She seemed composed, busy, and somewhat intimidating – a stark contrast to my shy 19-year-old self. Little did we know at the time that we were destined for a kind of soul connection. As the years went by, I discovered that this seemingly cool person was one of the warmest souls I'd ever met. We worked together, attended concerts, faced highs and lows like heartbreak and health challenges, and gradually grew dissatisfied with our roles at the advertising agency where we'd spent the last 5 years side by side.

Our days were a mix of autonomy, seminars, client interactions, and juggling the intricacies of order processing with production. Sounds good, right? Well, despite the apparent freedom, we were far from feeling truly liberated and content. The workload was overwhelming, and the compensation was less than stellar. With a mere 22 vacation days, it was pushing the limits. Falling ill was a tricky affair – you had to convincingly sound as sick as you claimed, a fact that was diligently verified through phone calls.

Even today, we still wonder why we put up with that.

The highlight of it all, however, came after an anniversary celebration. We - the employees, planned, organized, set up, welcomed guests, hosted, and, of course, cleaned up in the end. Despite being completely exhausted, we all felt it was a very successful event.

Well, almost all of us. Instead of a pat on the back for pulling off a great team effort at the celebration, our boss decided to give us a lengthy lecture about forgetting to sprinkle the glitter – which, mind you, we went out of our way to get. That was the moment – that pivotal point where my colleague and I both lost respect for the 'head honcho' of the company. The days that followed were just weird. After another miserable day at work, we met up with an ex-colleague who had already jumped ship. We drowned our sorrows, partied till dawn, let out all our frustrations. The morning after was predictably brutal. We were supposed to clock in at eight, but around eleven, we reluctantly dragged ourselves to our posts. Feeling like wrecks, we barely lasted two hours. It didn't take much longer for us to summon the courage to break free from the routine. Just like four colleagues before us…

…we called it quits.

Even if it's probably not the kind of story you're supposed to share, I'll spill it anyway. Did we have this grand master plan for our next big move?

Nope. The only thing we were sure about was wanting to keep working together, but now just for ourselves. Are we creating cool clothes, introducing custom toothbrushes, or launching an entertainment service for seniors?

Well, you know what they say: 'Stick to what you know.'

Okay, we decided to start our own advertising agency. We went to the employment office, got three months of unemployment benefits (yes, even though we quit ourselves, but that's a story for another time—let's just say, multiple sick leaves due to overwork and burnout). So, the three months of government funds became our window to launch our business.

Amid countless discussions on how to set up and build everything, Sandra's family thankfully allowed us to establish our business on their premises. I, as a complete outsider, was warmly welcomed and given the freedom to move around another family's property. In no time, I became part of it all, part of the family. Sandra's mom treated us to shared lunches and other wonderful things; it was like paradise (and still is today). After some talks with caseworkers who had helpful tips like startup grants and counseling for us, we put together our roughly 20-page business plan. By the way, that was necessary to qualify for the startup grant, which helps keep us afloat for a bit longer. Speaking of water, that brings us to the next crucial task for a new company – a memorable name and, above all, a logo with high recognition. But we didn't just want any old thing; we wanted sea/more. We wanted to tell a story. One of the many things that bind Sandra and me is our love for water and everything related. Maritime themes are perfect for a good story. Two now redheaded sailors ready to weigh anchor and embark on their own journey on the advertising sea.

Two of the most important things a seaworthy ship needs: a steering wheel (representing our creativity) and, of course, the anchor – our symbol for our own company. And so, 'Der Grafik-Anker' (The Graphic Anchor) was born. The advantage for us as graphic designers and advertising technicians is, of course, that we can create and produce all our advertising materials ourselves. This was very helpful for our budget. However, I would always recommend allocating some money for those who are not in the field. A professional corporate image is crucial.

Despite external uncertainties like, 'Friends shouldn't run a business together' or 'Money trumps friendship,' we now had a small 17m2 garage that needed to be transformed into an office. We had no clue about health insurance or taxes, always with a lingering fear of the financial burden and a bunch of other tasks ahead. With the support of capable acquaintances, dear friends, and our amazing families—who helped convert the garage into a cozy graphic cabin, encouraged us, lent a hand, and with the assistance of startup counseling—we got everything under control.

Our little garage graphic cabin is located in the beautiful Altmark region in Saxony-Anhalt. We love our area, our home, and deliberately chose a rural location. In the charming village of Jahrstedt, in the municipality of Klötze, my colleague's family had the mentioned wonderful domicile where we could set up shop. Here, we are optimally situated to personally assist clients in Saxony-Anhalt and even Lower Saxony. From the start, flexible digital work was important to us for personal meetings with clients. Since I don't live in Jahrstedt, and a daily commute would be quite time-consuming, we've created an additional advantage. We can easily serve clients in Berlin, Leipzig, or work from home.

Being completely location-independent for our graphic work, it's all a matter of organization, making unconventional work methods function well. While our clients have a meeting point, we aren't bound by specific hours.

On March 1, 2017, the big day arrived – the first official day of self-employment. After running some errands, we passed by a tattoo studio. A sign outside grabbed our attention: 'Today - Tattoo to go!' We kept walking, then stopped and looked at each other… Well, a few hours later, our own anchor – our logo – adorned our forearms. What's braver, starting a company together or sharing a tattoo? We did and still do both, without regrets, even after six years of self-employment.

But back to the beginning – there we were, the two of us, in a renovated garage that was quite presentable, with an anchor my dad had built, proudly displaying a G on one side and an A on the other. Considering many success stories began in a garage, we were confident we'd be part of that club. Admittedly, we're not at the level of certain search engine operators, but hey, who knows what the future holds.

After throwing an opening party, we got down to work. Without much thought, we continued at the intense pace we were accustomed to. But wait! We're the decision-makers now. Well, getting used to that took some time. We invested a lot of time, passion, creativity, and basically everything we had. Now, we could also take breaks for sports and prioritize our health. This self-employment thing is wild. We developed structures and our own rhythm, in collaboration with our clients, many of whom were navigating this new experience with us. In the initial months, we aimed to keep investments as low as possible. Collaborating with experienced partners, we could offer a complete package despite not having our own machinery. Gradually, as more capital became available, we acquired our own equipment to work even more flexibly. However, these tools couldn't fit in our 17m2 graphic cabin. So, an old party room at Sandra's parents' place was transformed. Instead of a sitting area, there was now a large high work table and rolls of film in the sunlit extension of the family home. Keeping costs manageable has always been crucial for us. We were grateful for the support from our startup center in Stendal. This support included a pretty exciting moment – we were the first female founders to sign a UNA-loan agreement in the presence of the Minister of Economic Affairs for Saxony-Anhalt. This micro-loan provided support to founders and had to be repaid within a year, allowing new entrepreneurs to benefit from it. The first two years were relatively calm, marked by healthy growth for a newly established company. By then, we had also submitted our first patent application for our own anchor. Certainly, not everything went smoothly on the path of development. Beginner's mistakes, such as errors in printed materials that we had to take responsibility for and pay for, or buying an old machine that didn't have compatible software for our computers. There were also external attempts to hinder us. Our former boss tried to intimidate us through legal means, preventing us from serving clients in 'his' city. However, the decision ultimately lies with the customer regarding whom they trust.

Fortunately, with good work, more and more clients from everywhere began to place their trust in us. This allowed us to survive solely on our own efforts.

Over time, we became bolder and decided to bring our big dream and passion project to life. In our business plan, we wrote about the desire for our own brand—a brand that reflects us, our taste, and creativity. In September 2018, we launched 'Kudda Klamotte.' Fairly produced textiles, preferably made from organic cotton, with hand-drawn and hand-printed designs. Pencils were sharpened, and several ideas were put on paper. Cool shirts were joined by caps, beanies, and whatever stylish sailors and landlubbers might need.

Then everything happened faster than you could blink… Through an acquaintance, by the end of September, we were already showcasing our Kudda Klamotte at a major motorcycling event, introducing our clothes and the recognition of the Graphic Anchor to the public. With two vans, too much decoration, numerous textiles, and stuff, there we stood. Personal product sales were a completely new experience for us.

It was a leap into the unknown. Not everything went smoothly, but it worked. People were excited, and we were overjoyed.

'It's evident that you're doing this with a lot of passion,' was one of the nicest compliments. By the way, at the end of August, none of what we sold in September was ready. To seize this excellent opportunity, we had to pull many all-nighters—searching for good textiles that wouldn't strain our budget, producing prints, and everything else. As beginners, one can quickly underestimate the time involved. However, a certain pressure always drives us to excel. So, for the event, we had different designs on various shirts, various hoodies, caps, and warm beanies that kept the ears of the visitors nice and toasty in the evening.

That inspired us - our Kudda clothes then moved into a small online shop that we operate on the side. Running a shop requires inventory, and for that, you need a warehouse. After a conversation with Sandra's grandma, we were allowed to transform the 'good room,' unused for a few years, into a Kudda clothes storage. Instead of a large wardrobe, there were now floor-to-ceiling heavy-duty shelves in the spacious room. Packed with boxes containing sleeping clothes, shipping cartons, and other goodies to delight customers. Initially, we were a bit ambitious with the inventory, but it's all part of the learning process.

Over the years, we've been to numerous events with Kudda Klamotte made by 'der Grafik-Anker.' We've met countless amazing people, and personally, I even found love while selling clothes.

Now, onto another quirky aspect of my self-employment that is probably a bit unusual. Our companies are in Jahrstedt (Saxony-

Anhalt), and I live 80 km away from there. I have a friend who lives in the farthest corner of Brandenburg. How do you manage all of this? I can say it works quite well. I spend a week in Saxony-Anhalt, meeting family, friends, customers, and my colleague. We discuss orders and plan projects. Everyone can also work from home or the office. Then, I spend a week in Finsterwalde, where I can calmly design and complete my orders, gain customers in another federal state, and provide personal support. Flexibility and good structured planning are everything.

Even when it comes to the topic of Corona, the setup of our business with established home office and digital customer contact has helped us a lot. Our customers could experience order processing almost as usual, without significant adjustments. We didn't have additional costs for working from home and luckily didn't suffer major losses in production. Like everyone else, we weren't spared from immense material price increases from our suppliers. However, by keeping our ongoing costs low through nonexistent loans, we were able to handle it. That's how we navigated through 2020.

But then something happened that we weren't prepared for. My colleague Sandra stood in the office with a pale face. She mumbled a few words and finally pulled a white test with two red stripes out of her bag, and no, it wasn't a positive COVID test. Pregnant, self-employed, and work for at least 5 people. What now? Do we need support? Is there enough money for someone on payroll? Are there even qualified people available?

'Well, a baby sleeps a lot, so I can work during that time.' Those words from Sandra were very, very optimistic. Unfortunately, we couldn't find anyone to hire for support. Sandra powered through until shortly before giving birth. Well, then… it was time for me and everyone around me to grit their teeth. Weeks with around 60 hours of work each passed by. Designing, writing proposals, customer meetings, preparing slides, coordinating projects with subcontractors, handling invoices, taxes, and, in between, moving. I get dizzy just thinking about it. But that's also part of being self-employed. It probably doesn't always go smoothly, but if you want to keep living your dream, sacrifices need to be made from time to time.

Sacrifices, like having no time for sports or lacking a healthy diet, are things I wouldn't willingly endure again. We're constantly learning, realizing that, as entrepreneurs, we need to keep an eye on ourselves. Managing essentially two businesses doesn't make it any easier to strike a balance between work and personal life. We're still working on avoiding falling back into old workaholic patterns, and honestly, we don't always succeed.

Personally, I think entrepreneurship comes with its challenges, but we do have control over most things. Often, people make comments like 'Well, being self-employed means being constantly at work…' but we don't see it that way. It's crucial for us not just to be entrepreneurs but also private individuals. We value leisure time, the privilege of not working on Saturdays or Sundays, ignoring the phone, and taking three weeks off in both summer and winter. Experience has shown that we can only lead and sustain our business well if we are doing well ourselves.

After some time, Sandra fortunately rejoined the crew with a new and unfamiliar addition – a tiny sailor in the Anchor Crew. Open communication and continuous development helped us navigate this new and very cute task. After numerous unsuccessful searches, we finally found Sonja – our first employee, a signage technician with over 25 years of experience. Hooray, things are looking up.

Now it's time for development and new growth. Well, almost. First, we have to deal with employment contracts, vacation days, salary payments, health insurance, and all those topics that distract us from the actual work. However, we've committed to becoming employee-oriented bosses, valuing and not exploiting the helping hand. Sonja now supports us with flexible working hours, 20 hours a week. She prepares graphics, labels vehicles, and takes care of customer textiles and other details. For those who work a lot, space is needed. With the help of Sandra's family, another room was created in the family house, which we were allowed to occupy. Our entire graphics, which we used to knock over while maneuvering through the workspace, now have their own space along with the plotter (machine for cutting graphics). This not only gives us more space but also improves our workflow.

We have become a well-coordinated team by now, and we support each other through personal problems. The loss of a loved one affects both personal and professional life. As employers, how can we assist? Discussions with the tax advisor led to a solution. Every employee can take a one-month leave from work and still be covered during that period.

That's how it should be…

With the introduction of Sonja, we not only gained two helping hands but much more. She introduced us to a former colleague, a master in vehicle wraps with extensive experience in self-employment. Strangely, we had never crossed paths before, even though his workplace is just a few places away. The chemistry was immediate. Initial joint projects ran smoothly, and we moved our vehicle branding operations into a large facility in Lower Saxony. Now, we can refocus on development and growth, expanding our services to include more aspects of wrapping and broadening our customer base. We handle graphic tasks that aren't suited for wrapping, allowing him to bring projects to life.

After a few months of collaboration, it became clear that another independent wrapper and advertising technician would join the hall. Now, we are a team of 5 experienced individuals in the advertising industry, each with our own specialization. There's simply something to be made out of this…

At the current time, we are in the process of establishing a center/specialized hub. Consultation, design, in-house production, and expert implementation – all in one place. In the coming months, the entire venture will be further defined, and Kudda Klamotte should also find its place in the development. Initial construction measures have already been initiated, creating a platform above the production site. We and our clients can oversee everything. Craftsmanship for presentation. We are curious about how everything will transform in the near future.

Looking back, it's somewhat peculiar to see what we have collectively created with wonderful people 'just like that.' Daily life often obscures the view of our experiences – what we have built together. We have not only evolved professionally but also grown immensely as individuals and, above all, as a cohesive unit. Colleagues turned into friends, friends into family. I am very proud of us. I am also very grateful that so many people with similar interests and, above all, a similar life philosophy, accompany me on this journey through entrepreneurship.

From earliest childhood, creativity has been a constant companion for **GINA UHRMEISTER**. What started as a hobby eventually became a profession and, according to many clients, a calling. With dedication and passion, rough sketches and ideas are transformed into graphics and various advertising products, allowing other businesses to present themselves individually and professionally. In addition to her daily work as a graphic designer, Gina is also taking small steps towards literary projects aimed at entertaining and inspiring people in the future.

Instagram: *https://www.instagram.com/der_grafik_anker/*
Website: *https://der-grafikanker.de/*

Instagram: *https://www.instagram.com/kudda_klamotte/*
Website: *https://kudda-klamotte.de/*

SABRINA PATRICIA

I remember the moment so vividly. It was a rainy Sunday morning in November 2015, and I had just started a new chapter of my life, studying at one of Europe's top business schools, Copenhagen Business School… and I was about to give up.

I wasn't going to give up on pursuing my degree, or an even better job than I already had, or a life that looked even better from the outside. No, I was going to give up on the chase of feeling fulfilled and happy. Because that just didn't seem to happen for me.

Caught in a spiral of blaming and shaming, my internal dialogue was as critical and judgmental as usual. 'You are asking for too much! What more do you want? You just need to be more grateful!'

The truth is, I had built a life that looked impressive from the outside: the business school, internships, and work in NYC and Dubai, a job in an up-and-coming Danish tech start-up, a lofty Scandinavian apartment, and a long-term and loving relationship. While all that sounds like a successful life, one that would leave you feeling fulfilled and happy, I did not feel that way.

Not even after all these years of therapy and self-help books and my never-ending attempts to figure out what else I needed to do. On that rainy Sunday morning, I felt a sense of hopelessness. It was time to give up and make peace with the fact that my yearning to feel fulfilled and happy was just not going to happen for me.

Luckily, and I cannot exactly tell you how it happened, but on that day, I ended up reading the book "The Untethered Soul" by Michael A. Singer. The first couple of pages pulled me in, and I couldn't put the book down. I read it in one go, which was very unlike me, and felt so inspired that I decided to start meditating. And THAT is when my actual journey truly began.

But let me start by giving you a bit more context…

While I had built this life that looked great from the outside, I grew up having a real challenging relationship with myself. From feelings of anxiety to complete panic attacks, to depression, and an unhealthy relationship with my own body. All while holding a deep conviction that there was something fundamentally wrong with me. In my behavior, that showed up as doubting and second-guessing myself, constantly attempting to please everyone around me, and feeling paralyzed when having to make a decision. Eventually, I spent about three months in a clinic for people suffering from eating disorders, followed by years of therapy. Therapy certainly got me to a place of functioning well in this world, but I never managed to fully dissolve the belief that there was something wrong with me. Besides my accomplishments, I wanted more. I wanted to no longer hate myself. I wanted to feel confident beyond the 'fake it until you make it'. I wanted to believe in myself. I wanted to feel excited about my life and where I was headed. And none of these accomplishments had gotten me to that point.

It truly was an exhausting journey of comparison, trying to copy what I thought those around me were doing, and of course, a lot of 'fake it until you make it'. Until that one rainy Sunday in November 2015, when I came across Michael A. Singer's book. A book that left me feeling so seen and heard in my experience. And let me tell you, feeling so deeply seen in my experience lifted a heavy weight off my shoulders. A big part of it was finally convinced that I was not alone in this experience, and it gave me hope. Hope that there was a way to navigate all these thoughts and emotions. Meditation was the starting point. Struggling to find my seat and sit up straight, I began to meditate and immediately made it an integral part of my life. The relief I experienced from it, the mental space it provided me with, and the clarity that began unfolding were what pulled me deeper into the practice of Meditation.

As I now know, this was only the beginning.

Meditation and Yoga helped me rewrite the relationship I had with myself, moving from self-hatred to a relationship that allowed for kindness, compassion, and trust in myself. If anything, this is what propelled me to where I am today, but let me not get ahead of myself…

Being deeply immersed in the practices of Meditation and Yoga, having attended a 10-day silent Meditation retreat and countless hours of practice and training, I naturally reached a point of wanting to share what I had learned and pass on these tools. I started building a side hustle of teaching Yoga, Meditation, leading Sound Bath Ceremonies, Retreats, and Corporate Mindfulness Events.

Besides that, I was still pursuing a career in Corporate, driven by my idea of wanting to be successful and what I – at that point – believed success to look like. That very belief and conditioning around success led me to take on a job in Berlin at a global tech company with all the perks, from coconut water in the fridge to pizza with the teams on a Friday afternoon. Given my education and career track thus far, it made sense and sounded intriguing. In March 2020, I moved from Copenhagen to Berlin and was off to a rough start. Just a couple of days in, we were all asked to work from home. At that point, I hadn't even met my team in person or furnished my new apartment. So, I ended up sitting on the floor in an empty apartment, not knowing anyone in the city of Berlin – but still thinking that this would only last us a couple of weeks and then we'd go back to 'normal'.

We all know how that went…

Besides coping with a global pandemic, I was quite frankly underwhelmed with the job I had taken on. I was – once again - disillusioned by the corporate culture, by the team culture, and questioned my role in all of it. In all honesty, I felt like I was wasting my time…and I could not help but feel like I was right back where I started in 2015: having built a life that ticked all the boxes but left me feeling deeply unfulfilled. Wasn't it the prestigious job title, the renowned company, the paycheck, the holidays, the lifestyle, and of course the greatly sought-after 'security' in life, that is supposed to leave us feeling accomplished and successful? Well, it clearly didn't work for me…

Thankfully, at the time I was offering private 1—1 Sound Bath Ceremonies and it seemed like this was something that a lot of people really wanted and needed at the time. Most of my private clients worked with me over a couple of months, and I noticed how with time these sessions took on a dynamic that I knew from working with a Coach. A new and different dynamic that I absolutely loved. To make it even better: I felt like I was actually good at creating a safe space for people to open up.

Shortly after, I had signed up for a training and certification program to understand the works of a Coach more deeply and to find out if it was truly something I wanted to add to my repertoire. At that point, I was thinking it could be a nice add-on to my already existing side-hustle. Stepping into Coaching, I felt something that was rather unfamiliar to me: a belief in myself and a trust that I was really good at this. A confidence that went beyond the surface. Outside of my full-time job, I started working with clients as soon as I could, and it showed me how fulfilling work can be. I was driven by the impact this work had on people's lives, the transformations they experienced, and touched by the connections that were created.

And all of a sudden, there it was, a wildly audacious idea: what if I were to eventually work only four days a week and dedicate an entire day to my Coaching business? I know, I know… not the wildly audacious idea you'd expect. But at this point, it felt like a massive stretch to me. Having been conditioned to believe that this job I had taken on was the path to success, to leading a life that I had imagined with the beautiful home, the travels, the lifestyle, I hadn't fully built up the trust and confidence that all of this would be possible outside of the corporate structure as well. That was only for a few lucky ones out there.

I needed another push. A push I got when a promotion I had been working towards and was promised by the manager, was not given to me. Feelings of frustration and disappointment built up, and I felt deeply unappreciated and went straight back to the underlying feeling of wasting my time. The difference this time was that I had experienced work that felt the exact opposite. Not only did my Coaching business feel more and more fulfilling, but it kept growing. Previous clients referred me to people they knew, and it felt like I was picking up some momentum.

With that sense of momentum, my vision for the future expanded. What if I were to start a full-time Coaching business? Could this work? Would this actually be possible for me? While I got increasingly excited about this idea and the vision for my life, there were a lot of people who felt differently about it. A whole lot of fears and doubts were thrown my way. I came to realize that I needed to be more intentional about who I share my ideas with and when I'd share them. I needed to remember that the feedback will inevitably include a lot of projections of that person's own fears and insecurities and not all of this was mine to take on. I had to become better at discerning what was constructive feedback and could guide me into deeper reflection and what was nothing more than another individual's projection. I also realized that I wanted to spend more time with people who were doing the very thing I dreamed of doing. I signed myself up for a global mastermind with other women leading their own businesses or wanting to make the shift. This was an opportunity for me to understand if this was truly what I wanted and get a clearer sense of what was required to make the shift. Essentially, I was learning from other women's experiences, their challenges, and hurdles and at the same time connecting deeper with my own intentions and drivers to identify my very own unique path. I let myself be supported even more and worked 1-1 with a Coach. Having worked with Coaches before and supported others in that role, I knew this was going to be powerful. Our work was not centered around the 6-Step-Action-Formula to quit the corporate job and build your own business. Our work was focused on my inner world, the beliefs I held, and limitations that kept blocking me. And there were a lot… the classic feeling of an imposter, the shame of wanting too much to deep existential fear around what if all of this would not work out. Working through these very natural fears also meant creating a new belief system and fostering a deep sense of trust in myself and life, a confidence in my self-leadership skills – essentially an inner toolkit that would support me throughout this journey and beyond.

With the gift of hindsight, I can see how the most important thing I did was redefining my beliefs around safety and security. Safety and security are one of our core human needs and through our upbringing and the collective, we are all being given a particular blueprint of how we get to meet and fulfill that need. For most of us, this is through a stable job, a regular paycheck, a steady home, and a committed relationship. And I was about to throw most of that out the window. I went through the process of deeply understanding what safety means to me and how I can meet that need for safety for myself outside this pre-constructed way of life, outside of what I was conditioned to believe.

This is when I started focusing on my financials. I wanted to build up savings that would allow me to continue leading life exactly the way I was at the time for 6 months. This to me felt safe – for 6 months I would know I am okay even without signing a single Coaching client. I also delved into a deeper understanding of regulating my nervous system. This work was not new to me given my years of practice of Yoga, Meditation, and Breathwork, and yet I came to understand the importance of this work at an entirely different level. What I had in mind was not going to be possible when tossing and turning at night, waking up with a body riddled with anxiety and a mind that was unable to focus. I prioritized creating a sense of safety and stability within myself, my body, my mind through regular practices of Meditation and Breathwork, through prioritizing sleep and rest.

Another aspect that I came to understand was providing me with a sense of safety was connecting to other people who were on a similar mission and path. I made that possible for myself by committing to long-term Coaching and reaching out to others with a similar mission through joining Masterminds, Group Coaching, as well as Instagram.

So finally, I get to tell you that, YES in 2021 I quit my job in tech and went all in on my Coaching business. The Coaching business also gave room to my aspirations to lead a life of greater freedom, time freedom as well as location freedom. It was also a personal revolution, a desire to break out of the constant hustle, the grinding and a yearning for a life that felt deeply fulfilling – a process of redefining success, where both needs and visions are met and fulfilled.

Fast forward to now, where I am in my third year in business, my life looks very different and, most importantly, it feels entirely different. I moved from Berlin to Cape Town, a place I kept coming back to ever since a high school exchange to South Africa in 2009, and continue to lead my Coaching business. From 2022 to 2023, I have grown my business revenue by over 400%, turning it from a cute little side-hustle into a business that sustains me and the life I am leading.

I believe that it was my redefinition of success, my deep understanding of Self paired with learning how to courageously and consistently move in alignment with my greater vision, that helped me create this amount of growth. Nonetheless, I want to be intentional about the way I share, because by no means was this an easy journey, by no means did that happen overnight. In fact, I was brought to my knees multiple times. My first-ever Group Coaching program flopped entirely. The worst possible thing happened: only one person signed up! It would have been so much easier if nobody had signed up, but in this case, I had to actually communicate to the client that, well, there is no group. Yes, I offered her to work with me 1-1 instead and it was a beautiful journey, but the feelings of shame and failure were strong and I wanted to hide away in my room instead and made me question my ability to not just coach people but run a successful Coaching business – two entirely different things!

I can honestly say that starting and running my own business is the greatest initiation into my own personal power but never has it been handed lightly to me. This is where we land back on the importance of the relationship you hold with yourself. If anything, you carving your own path is a journey of growth and constant evolution. There is no growth unless you can hold yourself in kindness and compassion while taking radical ownership over your actions. It is the continuous refinement of my inner world that allows me to lead life in alignment with my mission: to support visionary women in creating a truly rich life – inside and out. I do this through Coaching, Trainings, and Retreats that help you rewrite the relationship you hold with yourself and fully step into your power, actively leading life as who you truly are and creating the impact you envision. I walk alongside the kind of woman who has been living life dictated by expectations and pressure, outside ideals, and in the process has most likely created a life that appears to be successful, but she is exhausted. Because while she wants to hold the external, this woman has a yearning to lead a life deeply rooted in her leadership, impact, and contribution.

To me, it is the greatest honor and impact lies in the depth of the individual woman, to see more and more of their truth be reflected in how they show up in life. This, I know and trust deeply, has an unimaginable ripple effect. Women like that show up differently for themselves, for their relationships, for their teams, their organizations and leave an imprint wherever they go. With everything I have created thus far, my vision continues to grow and unfold in beautiful and surprising ways. I am driven by impact and so I am continuously opening my body of work to larger groups. I currently feel deeply inspired by a shift I noticed in 2023: an increasing number of organizations, small and large, begin to see the power of personal development and actively support their employees through Coaching and Mentorship. I am convinced that great leadership starts with the skills and tools to self-lead.

With that, if you are here to lead a remarkable life, a great business, a brand, I encourage you to explore the depths of self-leadership through the redefinition of success for you personally.

SABRINA PATRICIA, previously a corporate professional, has mastered the transition to becoming a professionally trained and certified, and heart-centered coach and mentor. Drawing from her own journey of resilience and self-discovery across dynamic cities like NYC, Dubai, Copenhagen, and Berlin, she redefined success for herself: now based in Cape Town, she follows her deep calling to support other women in unlocking their true potential, running her own coaching business. With a focus on mindfulness, self-leadership and inner transformational work, her focus lies in empowering women to embody their authenticity and lead lives of greater self-leadership, success, and impact.

Website: *www.sabrinapatricia.com*
Instagram: *instagram.com/sabrinapatricia.sp/*
LinkedIn: *https://www.linkedin.com/in/sabrina-klaubert/*

MARKUS WEINBERG

'It was the day of the massacre of Irpin and Buchta. With my translator, we stood just a few kilometers away, unaware, on top of a high-rise building, while on the horizon, the rockets and grenades could be heard and seen.'

At the beginning, there was a dream. I wanted to tell stories, make television, and shoot movies. I wanted to share adventures not only by experiencing them myself but also by letting other people participate. However, at the age of 14, I didn't really have a plan for how to achieve that. Television was scarce at home because, for most of my childhood and adolescence, we simply didn't have a TV. Consequently, I paid close attention to the medium when it was consumed at friends' houses, with family, or on other occasions – as you can surely imagine. That was probably one of the reasons why I was drawn to the medium of film. Another reason might have been that my parents pursued their climbing hobby somewhat excessively.

Growing up in an artistic and mountaineering family, I had to climb the rocks of the Saxon Switzerland from a young age. As various well-known mountaineers were part of our circle of friends, we often had film crews and journalists visiting, whom I followed attentively and with full interest. There were also lectures about climbing adventures from other countries, first ascents of new routes, and entirely unknown areas. Definitely enough material to dream about. Another incident: I met a group of wanderers who knocked on our door one Easter day in the Saxon Switzerland, asking for a place to stay overnight. Half the town had sent the small, odd group of boys to the climbers in the village, who would surely clear out the attic. They were right. So the somewhat soaked group with their sleeping bags and guitars ended up at my bedroom door on the attic. The reward for the sleeping place: a few fervently sung travel songs.

I was thrilled, and just a few weeks later, I joined the group for the first time on a large camping trip. From then on, alongside climbing, it was all about journeys, distance, and adventure for me. Every spare moment, I went on weekend trips, winter, Easter, or autumn trips with my wanderer group, and then, of course, the weeks-long summer trips across half of Europe or to South Africa. All boys between 10 and 25 years old, with backpacks, hiking boots, guitars, and plenty of songs in tow. A group that can be compared to scouts and is associated with the 'bündische Jugend' movement. Their heyday was certainly in the twenties. Our society owes them, in the broadest sense, youth hostels, the reform movement, and even the nudist movement. In other words, I lived the adventures myself since I was 11 years old. To capture these experiences, my summit book, which meticulously recorded every climbed route, transformed into a classic diary of my travel experiences. Additionally, my mother gave me a camera, and I began initially capturing individual moments on the 24-36 frames of rare film rolls –

including Corsica, Poland, Greece, Italy, and South Africa. At home, I continued attending lectures by Bernd Arnold, Kurt Albert, but also adventurers like Joe Bentfeld. I started giving my own lectures about my journeys – slide shows among friends and family.

Let's put it this way: I still had energy left over. Especially during puberty, it had to go somewhere. Alongside climbing, more (endurance) sports slowly but steadily made their way into my life. The separation of my sports-oriented parents and their respective new, also sports-oriented partners, expanded my horizons when it came to sports. Climbers were certainly considered alternative in the mid-90s. With their tattered clothes and not far from vagrants, they often spent the night under rock overhangs in so-called 'Boofen'; a Saxon word that means 'sleeping under the rock overhang' as a verb and refers to the sleeping spot under the rock overhang as a noun. Close to the existence of the wanderers. Another characteristic of climbers back then: They were secret triathletes, riding their bikes to the mountains, running on narrow paths to the rock, and then climbing. Or sometimes running first, then climbing, then swimming... or... What I'm trying to say is that it wasn't just about climbing. Hiking, skiing, cycling, paddling, and just about every other outdoor sport were welcome diversions.

Where there's sport, there's also a desire to measure: who is the best, the fastest, the highest, the boldest? This is also eagerly reported on, including within our circles. Participating in popular competitions in climbing, cycling, running became a beloved change of pace from the hiking trips and the almost daily nature experiences at the rocks. One of the journalists who liked to report on the entire alternative scene and lived (part-time) in close proximity to my parents even had a whole TV show on the topic: BIWAK (bivouac shelter or bivvy). I did my first school internship in 8th grade with him, which was an exciting experience. Besides reading letters from viewers, planning the show, cycling the routes, scouting, watching the filming and editing, and finally admiring the finished result on television, I now knew: This is what I want to do in the future. As straightforward as the desire was, the future realization was filled with detours. The path to becoming an editor, journalist, and filmmaker was long. In between came school, political engagement, the wanderers, enthusiasm for competitive sports, a year-long journey around the world, civil service, studies, a career as a professional athlete, founding a company, falling in love, having a child, separations, a brief permanent position, and finally, the first steps towards realizing my dream. Looking back, everything is naturally interconnected, including trials and tribulations. But it wasn't quite as simple as that.

Experiences and interesting people around me were never lacking. It became and remained a need for me to tell these stories. But before that, there was a completely different point: I just did it, started, didn't see the obstacles, but rather the expansion of horizons, the potential experience. And in doing so, I grew. I never waited to be good enough first. If a chance or opportunity arose, I seized it and became better along the way. Where others hesitated, I tried and learned. Like in science: if an experiment didn't work, you knew that it was a dead end, that path didn't work, and you explored another one until you found a solution. Like with my later mountain bike guiding company, TransOst. The routes that my father, my business partner, and I explored were created by riding countless trails and paths, to eventually offer a beautiful, functional route. How often did we get stuck in thickets, dead ends, or impassable paths and had to turn back, start anew – the experiences were unique and often the most beautiful and formative. Exposing myself to these detours was and became for me the essence of a rich life. The highway, the direct route, seemed increasingly boring to me. The consequence of this hunger for experience was that my desire to make films initially took a back seat. Unconsciously, I didn't want to take the paved highway. Honestly, I also lacked the confidence to proudly drive my Trabant next to the Ferraris. But the idea of now having to limit myself when life is full of cherries didn't sit well with me. Or in other words, I simply hadn't done nearly enough to pursue the path of filmmaking. It wasn't time yet. A glance at the curricula of renowned German film schools translated to: If you already know everything, then you can apply. And I knew nothing. Only living the experiences that were gladly filmed and reported about. So, I could do something after all, but at that time, without an idea of how to really bring it all together.

By now, I had focused more on sports. While climbing was my parents' hobby that shaped my entire childhood and adolescence, cycling thrilled me even more. Not just climbing to summits and gazing into the distance. No! I wanted to ride into the distance. Towards the horizons I could see from there. Cycling suddenly expanded my range of movement and made me independent of the almost non-existent public transportation in my 200-person village, surrounded by rocks, where I grew up. I also enjoyed racing, and the nearby town where my father had moved had a cycling tradition with several races throughout the year. Shortly before, a certain Jan Ullrich had won the Tour de France and an Erik Zabel had won countless stages, which also revitalized the local cycling club and led me to obtain a racing license and soon join the junior Bundesliga team of my state capital. A well-intended hint in the curricula of those film schools suggested that a foundation in humanities studies could be quite helpful for a future film application. This prompted me to take a closer look at those subjects. I chose political science, modern and contemporary history, and sociology. Since I had already traveled as a hitchhiker, hiker, and cyclist to various countries as a teenager, served as a student representative in school, had a strong interest in history, avidly read newspapers, and devoured books, I thought that this combination of majors wouldn't be a bad idea. And it gave me plenty of freedom to pursue my increasingly solidifying passion for road cycling.

That had one downside: such a degree involves a lot of writing – not exactly my forte. Not because I didn't know what to write – I wrote a lot – but because my spelling was rather poor. It's still a mystery to me how I managed to pass my high school diploma, let alone with German as a major. It was unimaginable for me to ever work for a newspaper or do anything related to writing. Fortunately, I kept meeting people who were willing to help me, sit down with me, take the time, give me chances, or throw me into the deep end, thereby fueling my ambition. I only learned to write properly during my studies. I felt like I pounded every word into myself, using mnemonics, photographic memory, etc. Even today, I have to think about many words, and it's not easy for me, yet I have already been published in many magazines, contributed to books, and written countless articles, texts, synopses, treatments, or advertisements. At some point, I began to see this weakness not as an obstacle, but as a task, a challenge to embrace. Nonetheless, there were many situations where I felt endlessly embarrassed when I misspelled something again. Whether it was at school on the blackboard, on an invitation card, later at university, or today when I'm asked to sign a book and write a dedication. Especially in the latter situations, the insecurity returns, simply due to the pressure when someone is watching and it has to be right. My strategy now: I casually ask my counterpart how it's spelled again, as if it were the most normal thing in the world. It doesn't always work, but mostly.

Even today, I always have my texts proofread before they see the light of day. This episode doesn't stand in the way of my dream of storytelling. It's a strategy that can be applied in many areas. Because one thing was clear: I could tell stories, and film became my preferred medium for storytelling. Of course, I quickly learned that almost every story needs to be written down on paper before it's captured with 25, 29, 50, 60, or more frames per second and later flickers through television screens, movie screens, computers, or phones. Before I could enter the world of film, I needed several parts of a ticket that had to be put together first. The result of not taking the straight path. The first part was: having my own unique story, then being able to show a completed degree, and ultimately having a personal contact who was willing to help me. That was my individual cocktail to be allowed to start with news reports on television as a career changer. From my extra time as a professional cyclist and an extraordinary professional cycling race in Burkina Faso, my first television story was born, facilitated by my former internship supervisor nearly two decades ago. The fact that I was allowed to stay at the station and grow, to make more and different contributions outside of sports, was also thanks to my completed studies. Everything served a purpose. I learned for my part: You don't have to be the best in all areas; being good enough is sufficient, being able to finish things, combine them, find the special, be connected, and have the courage to pursue your own ideas. Again and again, I see people who are much better than me fail at this.

For me, it was an opportunity that I seized and then as quickly as possible: observe, understand, imitate, improve, and/or find my own style – to become good. Often enough, I also stumbled, just like I did with spelling earlier. Mistakes were embarrassing, but they often led to the steepest learning curves. It was the same with television. Sure, there were and are always people who are reluctant to help newcomers, the untrained, but fortunately, there are others who see potential in exactly that and distribute opportunities. My treasure trove was the multitude of experiences on my paths and in various activities. These stories, approaches, and contacts that emerged from them just needed to be channeled. The beauty of it was that once again, there were people who helped and supported me. And for that, I am humbly grateful. The same goes for founding my company. My time as a cycling professional was now behind me, yet I still regularly rode my bike and started racing again purely for the joy of it. However, now it was more mountain bike races and fewer road races. For some time, I had been volunteering in my former club to help organize a prestigious traditional race. To finish my studies, I earned my money as a freelancer in the field of trade shows, stage, and event technology. I worked with a great team of people at theaters, festivals, and all sorts of other events, enjoying excellent cultural events, concerts, shows, talks, trade shows –

everything you can imagine. The work was almost incidental to me compared to my curiosity about the people I met and the experiences I had. Nonetheless, it can be said that I now also had expertise in event organization and technology.

From this background, in my final year of studies, an entrepreneur and race organizer approached me, asking if I wanted to help him develop a race as well. Without hesitation, we founded what's called a 'One Euro Company,' a UG (entrepreneurial company with limited liability), the little sister of GmbH. Even though the collaboration was not meant to last long, it opened up a world to me that I hadn't planned on entering – that of an entrepreneur. Although I probably only truly learned the latter when I filed for bankruptcy exactly 10 years later. Through the founding, the opportunity arose for me to implement my own ideas independently, to experiment, and to find out what really suits me and what doesn't. So far, I've done things that interested me and brought me joy and fun. Now, a whole slew of obligations was added, learning what simply belonged – and I don't just mean taxes, but also financing, permit applications, and so on – let's just call it bureaucracy. But I wanted to take responsibility. Back then, obstacles were thorny opportunities, and since I didn't just live like a student, but was officially still one, I managed with little money. I gladly paid the price of uncertainty. Therefore, not trying was not an option for me. There will always be a way. Since I never planned to run a company, but only looked to see if a project interested me or not and if I still had time resources available, my recently started media work continued as a freelance editor and journalist, as did my freelance work in event management when money was tight again. Now I was also racing, we had a child, and I shot my first short documentary – the best conditions for a crisis.

Equipped with my first earned traces as an editor, I sought refuge in my first and so far only permanent position as a journalist for the Dresdner Morgenpost, which was undergoing a transformation or rather a renewal. It turned out to be the absolutely right decision, allowing me to sort myself out without financial pressure and, above all, to take a big step in the direction I had secretly wanted since my youth. A new team was supposed to bring about a fresh start, especially online, and I was given the opportunity to report almost exclusively across media platforms and topics. This meant I could deliver photos, videos, and text. A friend at the time roughly told me that the learning phase was over. I understood and really threw myself into it. Because otherwise, these were areas of activity covered by three different people. Especially at the beginning, I was almost the first in the editorial office and volunteered for everything possible, had everything shown to me, wanted to and was allowed to be almost everywhere. From commercial shoots to demonstrations, interviews, documentary series, reports, traditional news, photo shoots, press conferences, shows, sports events, live streams, etc., and if it had to be quick, I gladly did everything with my phone. That was my world: diverse, colorful, contradictory, exciting, political, lively, and fast-paced. On the other hand, there were also guiding hands. How often did I have to rewrite texts until they were right? Was a film criticized, but also shown to me how it should be better next time? Or were hints given so that the next photo would be right? These two years were invaluable, a paid apprenticeship in real life without respite. The entire journalistic toolkit was handed to me, and I brought energy, enthusiasm, and topics with me and always had an appetite for the stories of the people I encountered. It should be noted that the time from 2015 to 2017 in Saxony was extremely eventful, also for journalists: refugee crisis, protests, right-wing shift.

During this time, my company continued to exist in a reduced form because I was aware that my dream would never thrive in a permanent position, and this was just a phase to transition back to independence. With the new input and energy from the job, I made another attempt, found a new business partner, and essentially re-founded the company. Why I did this, I'm not entirely sure myself. Probably because at that time, I still didn't believe I could make a living from filmmaking, and I thought that my own company would provide me with the security to preserve my independence, which I believed I needed for filmmaking. I only learned later that it could be different.

At the same time, a documentary film topic presented itself to me that I absolutely wanted to pursue, and I found a film production company for it. However, to finish shooting the film, I needed unpaid leave, which I didn't get. Since the initial period of transformation and renewal at the newspaper was over, the structures were solidifying, and some freedoms were lost, it was a good time to leave the safe harbor. Shortly afterward, I found myself on a search and rescue ship off the coast of Libya: My film 'The Mission of Lifeline' was made, screened in cinemas, and shown at countless festivals.

At the same time, we also collaborated with ravir Film to shoot an adventure outdoor film titled 'Heading East – Abenteuer TransOst,' about three cyclists participating for the first time in a bikepacking race, the 'TransOst Challenge,' which I organized with my company. The race took place on the route I had explored mainly with my father and my business partner David, following the mountain ridges from Bayreuth through Czechia, Poland, Slovakia, Ukraine, to the Black Sea in Constanza, Romania. These were areas where my brand TransOst offered guided mountain bike tours. The race was like the cherry on top.

With the release of the films, I started to be invited more often to give talks, whether on political topics or adventure travel. My personal circle began to close slowly, although I still didn't consciously identify as a filmmaker or could fully support myself from it. Up to this point, I implemented whatever came my way, even though I unconsciously started to pick up more and more film-related projects. Even as a company, we experienced a springtime with this tailwind, investing, growing, spinning ideas. We attended trade shows, I gave lectures, guided tours to the Black Sea, got to know the cycling and tourism industry in a deeper way, and invested every cent with my company. We felt we were on the right track. On the other hand, I also found great joy in giving back to sports and my clubs, something I could enjoy myself, by taking responsibility for events that otherwise wouldn't have happened. Often, this was not very profitable. Then came Corona, a sudden end. Overnight, everything came to a halt, and a wave of cancellations hit us. After the initial setback, the positive side emerged. I had never had such a clear desk, which released new energy for ideas. Namely, taking a proactive approach under the motto: where there's a will, there's a way. Not just letting everything stagnate, like many competitors did, but recognizing and seizing opportunities. We should organize the first two MTB races nationwide after the lockdown. It was possible, one just had to come up with something. We came up with new ideas. Two completely new brands, one in the gravel area and one in individual sports. We hired people. However, Corona was not over.

It wasn't just a springtime, but it had long-term effects that extended beyond the year. The entire booking behavior of our customers changed, ultimately affecting the entire market in the long run. Everything became short-term and unpredictable. Organization became much more complex, and people quickly learned that many things could be done alone, as the technology for it had long been available. We lacked the capital to sustain such a long dry spell and make our ideas profitable quickly. Now we not only had a travel sector that had been in deficit for almost two years, but also the new ideas that were supposed to propel us forward. COVID-19 relief covered only fixed costs and losses, but not our process of transformation and the development of our ideas to adapt quickly enough to the given changes. Ultimately, I ran out of steam, and the company ran out of money. COVID-19 was bigger than me. The mechanisms I had learned no longer worked. Pushing forward with new ideas only exacerbated the situation. Less would have been absolutely more here. After two years, I felt it, but didn't want to admit it yet. At the same time, something else happened in the film industry. Shortly before COVID-19, I met an adventure athlete at a trade show who wanted to complete the first triathlon around the world. We hit it off immediately and planned to make a film about his adventure. It became a journey around the world during the pandemic. When it felt like all borders were closed, we managed to circumnavigate the globe.

Our spirit: simply try, and if something doesn't work, find ways to make it possible – just as I tried in the company. The whole story of 'The Limit is Only Me' and my film about it became a success. Bestseller, cinema tour, festivals, Netflix. Even before that, I received funding from the Free State of Saxony for another film project in Kyrgyzstan, and more film commissions followed. Only time and energy became increasingly scarce.

To top it all off, a crazy Russian sent his troops into Ukraine. A country I had traveled through extensively by bike in recent years, where we offered mountain bike tours for our TransOst customers in the Carpathian Mountains. Already on the second day of the war, our company van was on its way to assist the first refugees. It was supposed to shuttle back and forth between the border and Germany for a few weeks. We provided people with accommodation until government aid kicked in. Shortly after, I accompanied and supported aid convoys with medication to Ukraine with friends, reported for TV and newspapers, and drove with the relief goods to the almost surrounded Kyiv, conducting interviews on site. It was the day of the massacre of Irpin and Bucha. My translator and I were standing just a few kilometers away, completely unaware, on top of a high-rise building, while rockets and grenades could be heard and seen on the horizon.

Another blow to my TransOst and the company.

First Corona, now the Russians. Internally, I knew that things were not going well for the company anymore, but I didn't want to admit it yet with my business partner. We made wrong decisions, had to invest more and more time for less success. With the film came success, but it also required more time investment.

My second crisis was approaching at a faster pace than I realized. By the end of 2022, it was over. I simply couldn't go on. My time account was depleted. Before that, I received a call for a film about the major watershed of the USA, of course, with cycling in bike-packing mode. Another book was supposed to be created at the same time. It was another period of introspection or a kind of escape, as I cycled through the Rocky Mountains for three weeks. Avoiding the decision I secretly already knew the answer to. When I returned home after a month, an appointment at the bank finally opened my eyes. The bank advisor asked me three questions: Do you believe the market situation will change soon? Do you think interest rates will fall? Do you still have the strength and energy to turn the company around? If you answer no to all of these, he suggested that we close the file folder immediately, even though there was a positive forecast for continuation.

It was one of the hardest but most liberating decisions of my life, in a place where I didn't expect it: the path to bankruptcy. A radical cut. All the bike races, TransOst, the other brands and events, the agency work – everything I had worked for with passion for years, I had to leave behind. I resigned from all clubs and relinquished all voluntary responsibilities. I needed a clean slate because the emotional void I fell into was larger than anticipated. Suddenly, the energy and drive within me vanished, as if the tank was empty. Like a great fatigue after years of exertion.

Fortunately, I had my films. The book about the last journey had to be written, a series of lectures was planned, and I received a training scholarship for my first feature film idea. That provided structure in the crisis. Unconsciously, I was already living in a world I had always dreamed of. Everything seemed to be in its right place: adventure travels, reporting on them, making films, telling stories, giving lectures. When I was then approached to appear as one of the headliners alongside the climbing icon Bernd Arnold at the renowned Bergsichten Festival in Dresden, it emotionally completed a circle for me. What I had dreamed of as a child came true – and then also with the companions of my childhood, with people who once ignited the dreams within me.

For the first time, I was now at a point where I could say: I'm only doing one thing now. Unconsciously, I had evolved into what I had dreamed of as a little boy – living and telling my stories, whether in film, book, photo, article, stories, or lectures. Looking back, I can still say: every detour was worth taking.

MARKUS WEINBERG studied Political Science, Modern and Contemporary History, and Sociology in Dresden. Growing up in an artist and mountaineering family in the Saxon Switzerland region, Weinberg traveled the world before his time as a student and professional cyclist, always bringing back stories. For the past few years, he has been telling these stories. He has worked as a freelance editor for MDR, as a video journalist, and as a print editor for the Dresdner Morgenpost, among other roles. Following his childhood dream, he has been making documentary films since 2014 and currently works cross-medially as a freelance editor, video journalist, and filmmaker. His documentary films are broadcasted in movies and various streaming platforms as such Netflix.

Wikipedia: *https://de.wikipedia.org/wiki/Markus_Weinberg*
Instagram: *https://www.instagram.com/weinbergmarkus/*
Facebook: *facebook.com/markus.weinberg*
YouTube: *youtube.com/@WeinbergMarkus*
LinkedIn   *linkedin.com/in/markus-weinberg-941562a9/*

https://www.so-geht-saechsisch.de/podcast/rad-mal/folge-2
https://www.so-geht-saechsisch.de/wir-sind-sgs/markus-weinberg

https://simonpatur.de/markus-weinberg-wie-wird-man-filme-macher/

KEYA MURTHY

It was too early for anyone to be up, especially those with a 9-5 job and kids attending school. The phone rang; it was a landline. It was my brother asking, 'Did you watch the news?'

'You know I don't watch the news.'

'There has been a terrorist attack. Go turn on the TV.'

Suddenly, I was wide awake, tuning in the TV to CNN on channel 32. In those days of Cable News and landlines, my brother, familiar with my house, guided me. I saw one of the Twin Towers up in smoke, a plane flying into the second tower. It was like a GIF image, the background playing in a loop while reporters covered the attack. The anchor in the newsroom repeatedly asked, '… what can you say?'

Everything else was a fuzz in my head. The untouchable had been touched. The USA, nestled between two great bodies of water with a promised "Wall" on the southern border 15 years later for added security, had become as vulnerable as any nation on the planet.

I once worked as a software engineer in the Dot Com industry. The CEO prioritized profits, and eventually, the company was sold to the highest bidder. Everyone, including me, left with a laptop and a pink slip.

My six-figure income plummeted to zero with the Twin Towers bombing on September 11, 2001. I had three children aged 7, 4, and 1. It's hard to forget a day like that.

When my daughter got off the school bus, she noticed, "Why is Mom's car in the driveway?" Opening the door, she saw my flushed face, swollen nose, and red eyes.

It's hard to forget where you were on that day. The next week, after dropping my daughter off at school, I was engrossed in my office searching for job vacancies on monster.com. Amidst the quiet, I heard some noise. My four-year-old had woken up and was waiting in the game room.

'Good morning!' I cheerfully said.

'Mom, I am so happy to see you at home in the morning," he smilingly said.

I got on the floor and scooped him up in my arms. 'Who needs a job?' I said to myself. 'I have my son happy to see me in the morning. I have kids to raise.'

That marked the beginning of my inspiration and the promise to never return to the corporate world or work for anyone else. I knew I would never give away my time to make someone else rich. After breakfast, I went upstairs and turned on the computer. 'Work from home. Earn $6000 a month!' An AD banner flashed on Yahoo.com.

I clicked on it.

Thus began my journey down the rabbit hole to make a living while raising my children. 'Work from home' was both a dream and a scam, a reality that has unfolded over the past 22 years. In this changed world, dream merchants and carpetbaggers abound, each promising you can 'have it all' by following their system.

Despite enduring hardships and challenges during my 22-year journey as a part-time entrepreneur with a full-time mindset, I'm grateful I never gave up. Anyone selling hope always found me as their first buyer, and I still am. It's perpetually the promise of gold at the end of the rainbow and light at the end of the tunnel. I boarded the train of working for myself and raising my kids from home, and it's been an arduous journey. I relocated across the country, from Texas to California, pursuing my dream. The path was filled with lonely days and long, dark nights. Four years felt like an eternity, navigating through the dark nights of the soul.

Divorce, a 'friend' scamming me out of $65,000 USD from my credit cards, two years of paying loans without personal gain, deception by spiritual teachers and mentors, unauthorized withdrawals by Bank of America, bankruptcy, multiple accidents, death, homeschooling, nearly facing homelessness, relying on food stamps – the list is endless of the horrors I endured.

Call it madness or brilliance! The dream of being self-employed and the allure of owning my time have kept me on this train of working for myself with no stations to exit. I've hired coaches from around the world, leading to coaching calls at odd hours – in the middle of the night or the early morning. Over time, I've studied and learned how to become more resilient – a one-way street.

My worst saboteur is perfectionism disguised as procrastination. I successfully slay this demon each time it creeps up, anchored to the smile of my four-year-old ingrained in my memory, repeating, 'Mom, I'm so happy to see you at home in the morning.' My response is, 'Who needs a job when I can be a full-time mom?'

I recall my boss's words, 'I don't trust you,' because I wanted to work from home. My boss prioritized profits and pleasing his superior over the personal needs of his employees. My mother once asked, 'What about all your accomplishments at the university? Have you flushed your education and work experience down the toilet?'

My parents were born in a nation under British rule – India, a former colony. Freedom was an unfamiliar concept on their own land. Their primary concern was simple: 'How do I find food today?' The notion of 'fulfillment' never crossed their minds.

Their success formula was straightforward:

1. Go to school

2. Get good grades

3. Get a job

4. Earn+Save

5. Get married

6. Buy a house

7. Have children

8. Raise your children

9. Retire

10. Grow old

11. Die

Period!

Anything else in life is a bonus. If you crave more, eat and drink more, visit temples, enjoy movies, socialize, talk, travel, and indulge. Accidents, sickness, and discord are unchallenged; professionals like doctors, lawyers, and financial advisors exist to assist in times of physical or legal trouble and guide financial decisions. I disregard the formulas my ancestors followed to live their lives. I've never encountered an elder genuinely content; those who appeared happy were often deemed crazy. I embrace the idea that 'Crazy is the new cool.'

My motto: Who needs normal? Normal is average and dull. I'd rather be awesome and crazy – the new cool.

If I can't live life on my terms, then why live? I once read: 'Most people are afraid to die but do not know how to live.' How sad, yet how true! As Jim Rohn wisely said, 'Money makes you more of what you are.'

Money is energy.

I've encountered many rich-poor individuals – all they possess is money and the illusion that everything is well as long as they have money to pay for it. Transitioning from working for someone to working for myself led me along a twisted, zigzag road—up and down, right and left, front and back, and even upside down. Yet, it continually brings me back to where I started in 2001 – my 'why,' my reason for being my own boss. Often, I felt like I was spinning in circles and going nowhere. Yet, I don't know how to stop or when to pause. It's an upward spiraling journey. It's a lonely warrior's journey, akin to that of many successful people who, like me, have relied on numerous coaches. While I've had a few assistants over the years, the experience often felt like a lone-wolf endeavor. Spending so much time with an assistant made me question why I was paying them to do the work I could handle myself.

Training an assistant takes time, especially when the work requires intuition and sensitivity. The paradox lies in learning to fly and building the plane simultaneously. My journey hasn't been for the faint of heart; it's strictly reserved for the Braveheart. My highest level of work is reflected in Braveheart Coaching.

This life, my flight into my queendom, is a journey I cherish. I love every bit of it. I've never stopped or paused because, truthfully, I've never had the option to stop. Assisting clients, writing, and connecting through speaking are passions that drive me, just as I'm connecting with you through the words on this screen or pages. Even yesterday, my daughter asked me, 'Mom, you are on so many calls every day. Why do you get on all these calls? Do they give you a high?'

'I get tired from the calls. I go to sleep after each call.' and, yet I get on the calls. Most of them aren't my prospects or clients, yet I talk to people on calls and listen to them. And, here's why?

I get to learn from listening to conversations. Humanity fascinates me. By our greatness, our insensitivity, our pride, and our follies. When people speak, I notice their vulnerabilities and their stage personas. It gives me the faith to continue my mission of helping people overcome their deep insecurities and self-judgment and live their best lives possible. It's not about 'if she can do it, I can do it.' It's not comparing or contrasting yourself or myself with anyone else's success. Though a full-time mom, a single mom, with no support from anyone whether financial or emotional, I knew and believed I had to do this on my own and come up with my terms for success.

There is no overnight success. When you see the bamboo, you don't notice the roots that have been growing underground for five years, before it reached its full height in a month. Yes, m'dear, that's how the bamboo grows.

I know that most businesses go bust in a year. When walking down streets in a downtown area of my city, I notice businesses put up their sign. In around a year, it's an empty space before some other sign is hanging on their door and window. Unless you come from a family of business owners or you have a sponsor or investors in your enterprise, it's nearly impossible to start and run a business and also raise children single-handedly.

Most people I know who are successful in business have their parents or partners supporting them either emotionally or financially in their business. It takes a lot of bile to succeed both in the game of life and as an entrepreneur.

The taxman will forgive you if, for five years, you make a loss in your business because they know it takes five years to start earning profits in a business.

I was not fortunate to have the support of any kind. My family was disappointed that I was not using my formal education in physics, mathematics, and computer science or my experience of decades as a software engineer to make a living. Even today, my well-wishers wonder why I do not return to the IT industry and earn a steadier income.

I knew I was psychologically unemployable by 2002. It's not that I do not like engineering or appreciate my mathematical abilities. It's just that I do not want to deal with the corporate culture and people management. That's why I did all aspects of running my business. Accounting, Administrative work, marketing, Sales, and Sales fulfillment which is working with my clients and being their best version of coach, therapist, and healer.

Today, my children are older. My daughter takes time out of her life and has taken over the accounting, admin, and technical work needed to run my online business. But I still need to and do stay on top of my game.

Whenever you pivot towards or because of new opportunities, you will have a fresh set of challenges. When flooded with doubts, the mantra that keeps me going is 'everyday in every way, I am only getting better'.

Life has hurled enough monstrosities my way to give up this fantasy of being 'my own boss' story. But, there is a higher power and force that keeps me going and on track. Each time I fall, I pick myself up and continue without spending too much time dusting myself off.

Each time I go to the sink to wash my hands, I look into the mirror and see my foe staring back at me. I wash my face, smile, and say hello to the eyes in the mirror looking back at me. My reflection favors me with a friendly smile.

I return to life where I'd left it before I needed to rinse my hands.

Often, I remind myself there's nothing wrong with the world. Whenever negative self-talk arises, I catch myself and change it.

When my inner monologue changes, I change my reality. It's hard. Yet possible. Never quit on yourself. The universe's job is to support the vibes you send out. When I am not nice to me, I attract those who are not 'nice' to themselves and me. Early on, I learned that no one owes me anything. Everything I need or want, I have to work for. The harder I work on myself, the easier my life gets. I have two spiritual teachers and one spiritual mentor. Investing in the first five precepts of the Buddha pay the highest dividends. Not to lie, steal, kill, get intoxicated, or be promiscuous. My greatest foe has been the one within me who isn't investing in self-care. Making myself a priority in still an uphill battle. Mental and emotional challenges are an everyday struggle. My only enemies are my ego and my belief systems. I grew up in a culture and it has its own list of values which helped in forming my Belief System. As a hypnotherapist, I know that my belief system creates my reality. Whatever reality I experience is one hundred percent a reflection of what I believe to be true. Every choice you make, each decision you take is governed by your belief system. It's your internal script that dictates your life. Reprogramming your subconscious mind is not an overnight process. It's as tedious as the wind chipping away a mountain to carve out valleys, gorges and canyons.

Changing your life script to change your life takes a lifetime. So, you may ask, 'Why bother?'

Here's the answer: 'Because it's your life and you care about it.'

When I was earning a six-figure salary, I would say, 'My life isn't my work, and my work isn't my life.'

As a light worker, my work is my life, and my life is my work. The better I get at my work, the better my life gets. The better my life gets, the more successful I feel.

In the end, it's all me.

My spiritual teachers gave me teachings that helped me connect with my higher self for direct guidance. My spiritual mentor uses the teachings of the Buddha to guide me in making healthier choices and braver decisions that keep my wheels spinning and me progressing in the journey called my life. Growing up, I often heard the saying, 'Pride comes before a fall.' Because I wanted to avoid falling, I refrained from taking pride in anything. However, a few weeks ago, my perspective shifted, and I began to view pride differently, realizing it wasn't necessarily a bad thing, contrary to my previous belief. Once, a seventeen-year-old high school football player asked me, 'So, if I can't feel pride when I do well, what should I feel?'

'Gratitude and delight are great feelings,' I responded. That made him smile. Seeing him happy, I felt good.

A few weeks ago, on one of my early morning walks, I had an, aha! Now, being proud, feels different from the word pride. Today, I associate the word pride with vanity and arrogance, while being proud means you are happy to be connected to someone's accomplishments. I help working moms find time during their day. And if you ask how one finds time, I have a story for you. Mona, a 55-year-old lady, was asked by her husband, who's retired, 'When do you want the kids to come over?' It was the 4th of July weekend.

'I don't want the kids over,' she replied.

'What? Why don't you want to be with the kids?' he asked.

'I never said I don't want to be with the kids. I just said I don't to entertain anyone at home. Let them invite us.' she said.

For the first time after having entertained the family for 30 years, she had four days to hang around the house with her husband, sleep in, spend time in the garden, rest, and relax guilt-free. The kids invited them over. They enjoyed a good meal and great conversations. This is one of the many examples of how my clients find more time by adding their names to their priority list. David, a 52-year-old, was afraid that on Monday, he would get fired. He was divorced and a father of two adult children. He came to me for confidence to face his boss in their Monday morning meeting. That evening, he texted me to say he didn't get fired. Six months later, he got a promotion. Next year, he went to a high school reunion where he met his future wife.

Anything is possible when you change your internal script. When you shift your belief system, you change your life. Each decision takes you in a new direction to a new result that helps you live a new life.

Another bank manager in her mid-forties came to me, all flustered, struggling with aging parents she could never agree with. Also, she had to deal with her ex and her older boyfriend. Working with me, she got herself promoted to the head of operations. A few months later, she realized that with a new position and pay, she had more responsibilities that she did not enjoy. She gracefully bowed out of the new position and bank and now heads marketing in a nonprofit organization. All she needed was one-on-one time with me to see all that she already had and heal her relationship with herself. She enjoys healthier relationships with her parents and her ex. She even got into an enviable relationship with a new partner. Today, she lives happily in two countries. Anything is possible when you take a step back, give yourself one more chance, and work with a mentor closely.

I hope my story of adventures and misadventures explains why change feels easier than transformation.

Transformation is the death of the acorn for the oak to be born. Transformation is the death of the caterpillar for the birth of the butterfly. Transformation is the death of your past for the birth of your future. Your past left you. Why let it live rent-free in your head and hurt your heart over and over again? Regrets, remorse, and resentments are all byproducts of claiming your past as a prison sentence.

I talk to groups and share how what they are looking for is already within them. All you need to do is look within before looking out. Looking within is a multi-fold process, where you look up and dig down. The higher you want to build, the deeper you dig. This internal excavation brings you closer to the gold that you are. The spark within you needs space and air to ignite into a healthy flame that keeps you warm and shines the light for you to march on and for others to find you and gather close by. My vision for the future is a healed world. Light from one lamp lights up a thousand other lamps that light up another thousand each. Living in a lighter world void of heaviness and darkness is my sacred dream.

All change begins with me. I claim my light.

KEYA MURTHY is a spiritual coach and founder of the Ventura healing Center, where she supports her clients in achieving their goals for personal growth, forgiveness and spiritual healing.

Website: *https://CoachKeya.com*
Email: *coaching@CoachKeya.com*

Free Facebook Group for daily inspiration
https://Coachkeya.com/friend

Facebook: *https://.com/lifepathguide*
Instagram: *https://instagram.com/coachkeya/*
TikTok: *https://TikTok.com/@thecoachkeya*
Youtube: *https://YouTube.com/coachkeya*
Podcast: *https://coachkeya.com/podcast*
LinkedIn: *https://linked.com/in/coachkeya*

TONI POSITIVE

I'm 52 years old, happily married, and a proud father of a twelve-year-old boy. I live in a rural part of Holland, approximately 40 km north of Amsterdam. I was raised in this area, and even though there's not that much to do, I love living here. It's great to go to the city, but it would be too much for me to live there. Music is a big part of my life, and it was definitely my first love. I started listening to KISS when I was eight years old, got into New Wave/New Romantic, and was heavily involved in metal by the age of 18 (booking shows/tape trading). I saw Agnostic Front (One Voice-tour) when I was 20 and was struck by it. I stopped listening to metal and sold all my records. I gradually started listening to more socially aware bands like Ignite, Gorilla Biscuits, Youth of Today. This sparked the fire to start a band by the age of 30. From there, my record label emerged and got me very busy alongside my normal job.

At the age of 16, the thought occurred to me to become a barber, but back then it was socially not very accepted to practice a 'simple' craft like hairdresser/barber; especially for a young male. This would now be classified as homophobia. Even though general thoughts about males in the hair business have shifted, I would still say there is some work to be done. Anyway, I was told I was a good student and forgot about my barber ambitions. I went to several business schools and graduated successfully. From there, I got my first job at 24 years old, and before I knew it, 20 years in corporate business went by. Fashion, cosmetics, bike parts, and medical equipment were the businesses I earned my money from. By the end of 2014, I was heavily struggling with my motivation. This already started in 2011 when a reorganization at the company I worked for made things very unpleasant. Most people thought I was a bit of a freak with my loud outfits and music, but I was very dedicated to my customers and never had any problems meeting sales targets. As a matter of fact, it was all just too easy. So I started a band, a little later a record label, and organized all sorts of events. People around me started asking me how I could juggle all those responsibilities, but I did not understand them. I was like, 'Why are you so slow?'

So after a 13-year employment at a company (Medical equipment), I left and had no problem finding another job. This lasted only for one year, and I left again. Once again, I could choose from several companies for a new job but all in the same field. Not having the courage yet to break completely, I chose another company in medical equipment and started again. Shortly after I started this new job, I was driving back home and I cannot describe it other than "my fuse got pulled out". All energy was completely gone, and I could barely finish the ride back home. Call it a burn-out or, in my case, a bore-out would perhaps be a better description. The HR manager of the company was very cooperative, but in the end, I had to acknowledge that this environment would not be something to work in for another 20 years. It had to be something creative and self-employed.

In 2014, I needed a break, and I will never forget when a dear friend and his family selflessly offered their home for me to stay. My body and mind showed signs that I had to change to another environment. This visit to my friend (500 km away from home) was a game-changer. We had some fun days, including a graffiti session with his crew. We knew each other since 2008 when a picture appeared on my record label's Myspace profile. The picture showed a HUGE graffiti piece of my label. I was instantly struck by the size of it but most of all by the sheer effort of using my label's name for such a burst of color and creativity. Back then, I had put a lot of time and money into the label and was about to throw in the towel simply because things were getting out of control. I can sincerely say that my friend's piece made my day, plus it gave me new power to rethink the situation and to become even more committed to the label. This resulted in more than 40 releases and counting. My friend's art is prominently present in both my living room and my barbershop. It keeps reminding me that it is okay to walk your own path and stay close to your personal taste. I'm telling you this because it's important to have friends around you can relate to, especially when you're trying to make a change.

Since primary school, I always had the feeling that I was different. I found out I did not like football or most group-related activities. Sometimes I wish I was a little bit more mainstream, but "fitting in" is a hard thing for me to do. Being different is cool once you find your calling, but you also have to be prepared to suffer the consequences, feeling lonely being one of them. At the age of 16, everybody was going out on the weekend, but I did not feel comfortable with booze or drugs. My peers seemed to talk about nothing else. However, once I started visiting concerts, I found my crowd. Through the hardcore punk scene, I found people that did not care about booze or drugs. I did not know there was a name for it, but it turned out to be the straight edge. For the past 16 years, I've been running Positive and Focused Records, and since 2016, Danny is my label partner. He is straight edge too, but both of us are not preaching straight edge in a religious way. Most of my friends are not straight edge. It's a personal choice; it simply does not appeal to me to lose control over myself. I had been drinking an occasional glass of wine but stopped completely in 2014. I think I can understand Ian McKay (singer of the band Minor Threat) when he says it never was his intention to start a movement. Some people tend to use it and pretend they are better than others. The message always appealed to me, and it was an eye-opener for me to discover. I will gladly talk about it when people ask me.

Back to my career change; at first, I was determined to play my part in the music business. But this turned out to be a hard nut to crack, especially since I had a family and a house that comes with bills. Through my label, I had built a network with quite a few contacts, and I really did my best to find a way in music, but it did not work out. The biggest part of it had to do with the fact that I did not want to make compromises. I wanted to earn money with the music I love; hardcore punk, jazz, or electro. I was at a turning point in my life and felt the urgency to do something with my whole heart. My personal preferences in music were hard to turn into cash, and I would betray myself if I chose a more commercial approach. I have mad respect for people in music who stick to their plan. Most of the time, you need a job on the side, which restricts you from fully developing your artistic path.

Still not knowing what to do, my father-in-law said I should cut some hair because that is what he did for 40 years. My 16-year-old came back to me, and I said, why not. Right at that time, the popularity of the barbershop 'Schorem' in Rotterdam was reaching a peak, and they got their very own documentary broadcasted on national television. 'Schorem' has had a big influence on the barber culture worldwide. They have become true rockstars but kept that underground feel to it. Their approach laid the foundation for my own shop and gave inspiration to build a little space full of music and oddities. When Bertus and Leen (owners of 'Schorem') paid a surprise visit to my shop in 2018, I was totally blown away. Since then, Bertus did my psycho quiff twice. My 2022 haircut was filmed, and it has 1.1 million views. Just imagine…

Going back to school at the age of 43 was awkward, and it surely wasn't easy. For the whole of 2015, I went to a barber-school, plus I tried to cut as many friends as I could at home. I had the great advantage that my father-in-law was willing to teach me while cutting my friends' hair. So I went to school and had my private teacher at home. But it all comes down to commitment; some fellow students had other priorities and fell through. I was determined to make a success of it, and I loved the creativity I could put into it. The craftsmanship of a barber is one of consistency in your work plus the ability to communicate. Together with a friend, we built my shop in our garage, and I started in January

2016. Helped with my skills to promote my record label plus some life experience, I made a plan to promote my barbershop and even made it to the biggest national newspaper. Keeping focus is probably key, and the first 20 years of working have been a great learning process. It really helped me a lot to start my current business, so it all had its use.

Not having good memories about all the sales meetings and targets in my former jobs, but one thing I learned from there I really need to share: Whether you want to sell a product or a service, you need to stay in touch with your audience. In my specific case, I cut hair, and customers probably want another cut after approximately 5 or 6 weeks. So why wait for them to call you up? Let's make a follow-up appointment right away. And that's what I do; nobody is leaving my barbershop without a next appointment. It saves me and the customer a lot of hassle.

Life is all about finding balance. This was always what my father taught me. When he suddenly died in 2018, it did not take long before I was having some doubts about my working schedule. My wife works on Saturdays, and so did I… this left us with no other choice than to hire a babysitter for our kid. I made a calculation and decided to skip Saturday and have a 4-day working week. I realize I'm privileged I can make this decision, but spending time with your family is really important, and I still enjoy this Saturday with my son.

So from 2016 to February 2020, things were great; lots of customers and only happy faces. I introduced my own line of beard oil, organized concerts, and did numerous designs of stickers, T-shirts, and other merchandise.

Then Covid-19 came around the corner… everybody did suffer in some way. Personally, I was acting on the safe side, so over the course of two years, I was closed for 24 weeks and did not cut hair or trim beards. Of course, this was unpleasant, but I had already cut down on costs like mortgage for some years, and this turned out to be very convenient in these uncertain times. I was infected with the virus in April 2021 and March 2022. My symptoms were mild, unlike my wife, who is still not completely recovered today. However, this was nothing compared to what was coming next…

Since May 2020, I was increasingly suffering from diarrhea. Blood and feces got checked several times, but everything seemed to be fine. Many other tests followed, and in a search to find out what was wrong, I visited many specialists in both regular healthcare and alternative healthcare. Then in July 2022, I finally had an MRI scan that showed something. After an endoscopy and biopsy, they found out I had a rare form of cancer inside my pancreas (NET-cancer). According to the specialist, the tumor had been there for 5 years at least but most likely somewhere between 5 to 10 years. Long story short; I had major surgery in December 2022, and the tumor was removed together with the head of my pancreas, duodenum, gallbladder, and a piece of my stomach. The process to get a diagnosis was a bumpy road, but healthcare in The Netherlands is fantastic, and the people that helped me in the hospital were amazing.

I've had two checks so far and everything is okay; no cancer cells found. Unfortunately, recovery turns out to be a slow process. I started cutting hair in February 2023 again and immediately enjoyed my trade very much; it really gave me a good feeling and once again confirmed my choice for this change of career. This motivated me to step up in March but had a relapse and was forced to take it easy again. This has now occurred several times, and I have to acknowledge that I am not at 100%. It is somewhere between 50% and 60%; which is not bad at all according to the specialist; but my head wants more I guess. Perhaps the hardest thing about it is to accept this and even to take into consideration that it might not get to the full 100% again. After the surgery, I was highly combative, and my main goal was to play live with my band. I managed to do this in April and July. Both gigs were great, but after the last one, I had a real scary relapse that made me realize I need to dose the things I do.

Finding harmony; possibly this is the lesson in life I need. Why am I doing everything in such a rush? In retrospect, I tend to do things in a very hurried and energetic way. With this, I mean everything. From doing the dishes to walking the stairs, wiping the floor to sending out packages and from performing on stage to even writing these words. It doesn't come from my parents who are the most laid-back people I know. Why do I feel this urge to do so many things and all in a hurry? Being a perfectionist also doesn't help much either. I now realize more than ever my former employers must have thought; let's give him some more targets; and I did not protest because I knew I would meet those with ease. But as a matter of fact, I was very slowly burning myself up. At first, I thought being a sales manager and leading the sales team would fulfill my dreams, but very soon I learned this was not the case. It did not come from my intrinsic motivation, and soon I compensated it with even more projects besides my family and work. The switch to become a barber was a great first step, but my illness last year showed me there are more steps to make. Live more in the moment. In business school, we were taught it's never enough and profits need to grow every year. Always making plans for more; it's what all managers are dwelling on. Most of the time it's just a hollow shell with not much depth and the real drive is material gain or growth for the sake of growth. In society, this has become the norm over the course of the last few decades. Lately, there have been a lot of signs this might not be the way for our future. I sure know it's not the way for my personal future. I'm not a fortune teller but I dare to say economic expansion and globalism is not the way for any of us. When the success of my barbershop came, I have to admit I did have those thoughts to expand. Get a bigger shop; hire new barbers; enroll the concept to other places. I am so lucky I followed my gut feeling and did not do it. Otherwise, I would have stepped into the same trap of corporate businesses.

Back to this urge to accomplish so many things. Of course, there's a certain degree of satisfaction when you release a record or create a new sticker together with a well-known graphic artist. But it's even so important to enjoy what you achieved, and I somehow forgot how to do this. In a wider perspective, you could say more and more people lost this ability. We are running around like madmen creating moments of short pleasure, but if asked "are you happy," only a few would say yes. It's been 10 months since my surgery, and I never would have thought I would still be recovering from it. It has made me hypersensitive to crowds, noises, unexpected events, and even normal family life. These never were my best features but are now being magnified. But I do try to embrace my recovery and see it as an opportunity to find harmony.

For sure it has made me a more open person. I firmly believe that change is good; as long as you focus on the new and not fighting the old. The change from sales manager to barber was very satisfying. It needed perseverance, commitment, and love. Now for an even bigger change; my recovery forces me to bear a challenge where I need to develop other characteristics and listen to my body and mind. It's probably the biggest change in my life but I will approach it with the words I choose as a name for my record label; **POSITIVE AND FOCUSED**.

TONI POSITIVE is father, barber, entrepreneur and adherent of the straight edge lifestyle. Hailing from the area of West-Friesland (NL), this late bloomer found his calling behind the chair in 2014. Coming from a high performance environment as a sales manager in the world of corporate business, he redirected his energy towards a creative profession, and built his own unique sanctum. In addition to this, he runs a DIY record label with 44 vinyl releases, including the long running Youth Crew compilation series, sings in a hardcore punk band, and recently emerged victorious from a battle with cancer.

Instagram:
@janpietjorisencorneel
@positiveandfocusedrecords
@urgentkill

Facebook:
janpietjorisencorneelHQ
positiveandfocusedrecords
urgentkillhc